The Efficiency Theory

Timothy Scott Archer

Manuscript
Edited by: Michael Aschenbach

ISBN: 1-4563-2007-6
ISBN-13: 9781456320072

Table of contents

prelude: Since the beginning of time, every being that seeks survival has learned to work with other living beings so that together they can adapt to their environment, improve their efficiency, and secure their survival. For simple entities, such as cells and animals, this task is instinctual and therefore automatic, but for cognitive self-aware beings like us, this task is much more complicated. The social aspect of evolution is suppressed because we are surrounded by internal and external factors that clog our psyches, and without a clear psyche, our social functions become inefficient. This social inefficiency affects every aspect of our lives by decreasing our ability to live happily and comfortably, and impeding our ability to extend and preserve life.

I have written *The Efficiency Theory* to identify the issues that are clogging our psyches. My goal is to show that by eliminating the complexities that are hindering our progress and replacing them with a more simplified approach, society will run more efficiently and our development will evolve much more rapidly.

Chapter 1
Social Efficiency

Efficiency is defined as the measure of effectiveness that produces the minimum waste of time, effort, and skill.[1]

Efficiency is a term that recently has come to the forefront of the scientific world. As the world struggles to accommodate the enormous growth in population and to manage the distribution of resources, the effort to make things more efficient has become increasingly more relevant. We talk about fuel efficiency in cars and energy efficiency in our homes. We strive to learn how to efficiently collect data, use space, recycle goods, and run a business. Nevertheless, somewhere in this vast search for efficiency we seem to have overlooked the most powerful set of systems and tools we have, ourselves. If we are truly in pursuit of maximum efficiency, we need to look at how efficient we are as a social whole.

Most people wake up each morning with several things on their minds, but efficiency is typically not one of them. Instead, each day our thoughts and rituals are predetermined by our basic instinctual imperative to survive. According to renowned psychologist, Abraham Maslow, we have a general 'hierarchy of needs' we must fulfill.[2] Our first concern is immediate survival, so we must find something to eat and drink. Then, we must prepare for our future survival and the numerous factors that go into sustaining our lives. We need to clean ourselves to prevent illness, prepare for and obtain work so we can earn sufficient income to provide food, shelter, transportation, and entertainment for our families and ourselves. We also have to prepare for old age, when we will be faced with medical and financial strains that occur as our bodies break down and society turns their back to us. Since these issues are so important for our survival, they tend to consume our daily thoughts and habitually train us to focus on a narrow chain of events, leaving our efficiency unconsidered.

Our minds are then further clouded by social factors outside our control. These factors produce deeper challenges to both our daily imperatives and overall efficiency. Such challenges include the constant social, political, and economic volatility throughout the country. We have an economy that deflates and inflates like a balloon ready to pop. We have political battles that divide the country like two sports teams playing against each other, rather than binding us together to work as a unified force. We face terrorism and other crimes that constantly detract from our further progress.

Such volatility shows how inefficient our society really is and severely hinders our collective performance and future stability. It drags our attention even further away from efficiency by making our daily imperatives more challenging, thus requiring more attention on survival and less on efficiency. If we are to fix these problems, people must understand that this situation is counter-productive, and by improving our efficiency we will decrease this volatility and all of the imperatives for survival will become simple.

In 2001, I was one of the millions of people who felt the economic shock wave that resonated from the attacks on the World Trade Center in New York City. As a young teacher, I was stuck futilely searching for a job anywhere in the US. This was a pretty disappointing circumstance, considering how often teaching is advertised as a "secure profession." School districts suddenly froze all hiring throughout many states and even started cutting back because they did not know how long it would take for the economy to recover from these events. This was mirrored throughout the country in many other sectors as the markets tumbled and the economy continued to struggle.

After several months of tedious searching, I was eventually able to get my foot in the door, but only in a very economically deprived area, where most teachers would not want to teach. This shocking reality was the first of many wake up calls that demonstrated how the inefficiency of our society, and the systems that govern us, have led to such vulnerability.

In the years following these attacks, the US economy and society together slowly wobbled their way back to a reasonably stable condition. However, not even a decade later, we would again prove to the world how grossly inefficient our system really is. During the last few years of this decade, the economic impact of our inefficient system led to a collapse of several of the richest and most powerful industries in the world. In every industry from the housing market to the automotive industry, to banks and other major and minor financial institutions, the economic shock wave crippled the workforce at every level. From day laborers to Fortune-500 executives, jobs dissolved across the nation causing our economic, social, and political clout to take a major hit.

So why is it that, while our country arrogantly touts the greatest economic power in history, (boasting a GDP nearly three times that of the second wealthiest country, according to World Bank data)[3], we continue to find ourselves falling into extreme social turbulence and economic instability? Why is it that we continue to waste the skills of millions of people, find the gap widening between rich and poor, see the middle class falling closer and closer towards poverty, and continue to develop a culture of increased bitterness and distrust? Ladies and gentlemen, it is the inefficient system that we live by that not only causes these problems but also perpetuates them.

Let us look at where this inefficient system has taken us. Here we are again facing an economy that must freeze hiring, make millions of cuts, and scramble with various plans that borrow money in hopes of getting us back on our feet. According the Bureau of Labor and Statistics, the United States unemployment rate has hovered between 9% and 10% over the greater portion of 2009, peaking out at 10.2% during the month of October.[4] It's important to point out here that this statistic doesn't even include millions of people who are unemployed, but not claiming or denied unemployment;

those who are self employed; small business owners who have closed down and are now unable to make money; and real estate agents who can't claim unemployment nor are they able to sell a house.

The reality is, our rate of "unemployment," or should we say "work force inefficiency," is much higher. Several publications address this issue they call "hidden unemployment."[5] Hidden unemployment includes part-time workers who lose their jobs, discouraged people who have given up looking for jobs, and other unaccounted-for unemployment. Between figures the public is told via the media, and more realistic figures that include hidden unemployment, the differences are significant. The Bureau of Labor and Statistics had the standard unemployment rate for December 2009 at 10%. However, when accounting for temporary jobs lost and part-time workers, the number jumped to a jaw dropping 17.4%. Though these numbers still do not account for all the unemployment in the country, they are certainly more accurate.

Another issue the economy has created is discouraged workers. We have businesses cutting people's pay while forcing them to work longer hours because they need to save money and they know their employees have nowhere else to go. This is forcing productivity to drop drastically. No longer can a person focus on a certain skill set and be as efficient and productive as possible in that skill. Now employees are forced to wear multiple hats, being an accountant manager, front desk help, and running errands for the company, which makes accomplishing any single task much more difficult.

To illustrate how bad these issues have become, I would like to introduce you to a few people who represent what millions of others across the country are facing. The first is a man named Jim. Jim has a Ph.D. in Educational Philosophy, a masters degree in Administration, and a bachelors degree in Social Science. He was recently forced to return to the U.S. after teaching at an American school in Dubai for five years because enrollment in the international school system has taken a drastic fall. Since businesses have been forced to cut positions, cut costs, and focus more on domestic problems, they are sending many of the international workers and their families home, leaving Jim without a job.

When he returned to the U.S., he found no relief. He was left jobless as he faced school districts with tens of thousands of layoffs and no sign of rehiring. Though he is highly educated and has work-related and life experience that trumps that of most people in his profession, at the time this book was written, he was on his sixth month of doing odd jobs while trying to make ends meet because no jobs were available. Every interview he did manage to find has come with an apology and explanation that several hundred people applying for each position makes the choice very difficult. Only an inefficient system would allow someone with Jim's extraordinary knowledge and skills to be wasted.

John is another person I would like to introduce you to. He has a bachelor's degree in Human Resource Management. After tens of years of managing construction sites in various states, he is now left working as a sales representative for eight dollars an hour. He faces losing his home and has decided that now may be the best time for him to go back to school and work towards his master's degree.

He told me a story about his visit to the academic advisor's office that left him a little discouraged about returning to school. He explained that, as the advisor and he were discussing educational options, she pointed out to him that the office of the academic advisor had one opening that paid ten dollars an hour, at the beginning of the previous semester. She said they had over one hundred applicants for that position and the saddest part was, of those one hundred applicants, only three did not have a bachelors degree or higher. That means our economy has come to the point where highly educated and experienced people, people with extraordinary skills, are fighting over a single job explaining academic programs to people for ten dollars an hour. This again is a gross waste of effort and skill.

Then we have Betty. Betty has a master's degree in Architecture and twelve years of experience. She was one of the fortunate people who did not lose her job during the economic downturn. However, she still has a story to share about the difficulties we are facing. Though she retained her job, it did come at a price. Her boss instead fired three others in the office and now requires her to take on all of the responsibilities of the previous staff members as well as her own. To make things even more interesting, her boss also cut her wage by forty percent. This means Betty essentially has four times the responsibility she had before and is only being paid sixty percent of what she was making before they were fired. She explained to me that not only is she unable to keep up, but she finds herself spending more time running errands for the business, rather than using her expertise.

Sadly, these three examples are only a few of the millions of examples throughout the nation. What is even more unfortunate is that society did not have to come to this. All of these problems are a direct result of a system that is extremely misleading and inefficient.

One drawback is that our system focuses on **resilience** instead of **efficiency**. Let's really think about that for a moment. Our government, political heads, and media often tout the resilience of the American people and of our economy, but resilience is only necessary for something that is not stable or efficient to begin with. Resilience is essentially the ability to fail, to have something break, and then to build it back up again. That is a terribly inefficient system to strive for. Massive amounts of time, effort, and skill are wasted trying to pull our economy back to where it was originally before it was broken. When such damage occurs to the system, it invariably results in massive program cuts, job losses, and increased social unrest while plans are put in place to help society catch up again. Relying on resilience to fix problems is a fundamental flaw that only perpetuates problems and produces further inefficiency.

The inefficiency in our system is easy to see when the numbers are staring you in the face. The unemployment rate may be 25%, 10% or even 5%, but that number represents only one small aspect of our social inefficiency. We waste massive amounts of time, effort, and skill in political maneuvering that accomplishes nothing, but a symbolic claim to whose political ideology is deemed more important. We waste even more on building copycat products, producing useless tools, and tearing down and rebuilding the same things over and over again. We foolishly waste our most important resources: skills, abilities, and knowledge by turning our backs on our aging population, deeming others unfit to work, and perpetuating inefficiency with a broken education system.

The good news is that it does not have to be this way. The Efficiency Theory presents an evaluation of the overall efficiency of our social infrastructure and offers some solutions that correct the problem at its roots. Some of the concepts offered may appear absurd at first, but after careful consideration, I am confident most readers will realize how necessary they are to build a truly efficient society. The topics I address include such social challenges as crime, education, economics, politics, and multiple sub-issues related to these challenges. The book also looks at the psychological and sociological influences of propaganda, marketing, religion and other factors at the foundation of our social development. Where each of these topics are discussed, I will offer theoretical solutions to the problems analyzed. While these solutions may not be absolute, they should be considered a strong basis for reforms that must take place to mend the many social problems created by inefficiencies in our present society.

The primary goal of this book is to provide an ideology for a society that runs so efficiently that inequalities of power are neutralized, bureaucracies and politics are no longer necessary, crime and unemployment cease to exist, and a truly harmonious and free society can flourish.

As *The Efficiency Theory* unfolds, it will become apparent how society can function better, wasting far less time, effort, and skills by allowing people to do the things they love to do, restructuring how things are done, and compensating people fairly. It offers insight into how life can be when people understand how interrelated they are, embrace their passions, and bring balance to their lives by fulfilling their purpose.

Opening Our Minds

The first step to improving our social efficiency is to open our minds. We must realize that our immediate response to any idea is based only on what we currently know, learned through the familiar system in which we are trained. Something that is unfamiliar is not necessarily wrong; it is simply not yet understood. Not long ago, people believed the world was flat until a crew of men had the audacity to step outside what was accepted as truth and risk their lives to try something new. Some people may consider the ideas proposed in this book insane, because, like those who believed the world was flat, society has conditioned us to believe a certain way. Today, I challenge you to open your mind and set sail with me to discover how life on this planet can become the harmonious place we have only dreamt of, a place where all human beings are placed on the same field and can truly become whatever their hearts and minds can imagine.

As we begin this journey, it is important to look at what is not working, why it's not working, and how we can make it better. As the saying goes, "If we do what we have always done, we will get what we have always got." For a long time, we have been living by the same ideology, doing what we have always done. The tragedy is that, in our arrogance, rather than trying to improve, we have spent centuries trying to spread our way of life around the world. However, we rarely take into account that perhaps our way may not be what is best, considering the great depression, multiple recessions, high crime rates, and the over-worked, over-stressed feelings we have developed.

Interestingly, when surveyed on quality of life, the U.S. barely ranks among the top 15 developing countries in the world. According to the *Human Development Index* reported by the United Nations[6], and the *Social Capital Achievement* evaluation provided by Caux Round Table,[7] most of the top ranked countries are European countries where crime is low and quality services are provided for all of their citizens. Also, according to the International Labor Organization, the average U.S. worker puts in more hours at work than any other developing country in the world.[8] These European countries, such Norway as and Germany, tend to be more productive, work less, and have a much higher quality of life with happier citizens. Though a common factor among these nations is Socialism, I do not advocate Socialism by any means, because as wonderful and efficient as life is perceived in some of these countries, Socialism has several aspects that are very inefficient and our objective is ultimate efficiency.

Nevertheless, to do something different from what we have always done will take courage. We must step beyond things we know, and strive for something more. This is not an easy task because, whether we realize it or not, we are all products of social conditioning. This conditioning has trained us to believe we are doing the right things, and that, if it is not working, it is because we are not trying hard enough. We are not taught to question the system that creates and exacerbates these problems, but to question our work ethic and ability to use this system that has been set up for us

Social conditioning works like this: Most of what we believe is what we have been taught to believe by family, friends, schools, churches, politicians, and other people who have influence over our lives. Even our experiences, which grant us the truest form of knowledge, tend to be overshadowed by the teaching of others. Every book you have read, every class or seminar you have taken, and every boss who has shared with you what they believe have influenced your beliefs, just as their beliefs have been influenced throughout their lives.[9]

Once we realize this, we can see that all beliefs are nothing more than concepts that have been passed on from generation to generation. With this in mind, we can begin to look at all concepts, theories, ideas, and beliefs from a less biased perspective and come to a more thoughtful conclusion about what we believe for ourselves. Considering this, let us begin our quest with an open mind and see what we can do to create a more efficient society.

Our Founding Fathers Miscalculated

One of the greatest virtues of our founding fathers was the foresight they displayed when designing the laws that govern our great country. This foresight is demonstrated in the way the original laws of the land were broadly written, so that they could evolve over time, be interpreted by judges, and be adapted to an ever-changing society. These men understood social and political evolution and they wanted to allow a means for the laws to change as society evolved and changed.

Though this was a wise consideration, they severely miscalculated. These wise founders did not sufficiently anticipate the selfish, power hungry, and wealth dominated leadership our time was to endure. These great men somehow overlooked the potential for future generations of leaders to take advantage of this ability to change laws in a way that would suit their best interests, rather than the best interests of the majority of the people in our society. They also did not foresee the influencing power of propaganda, politics, and bureaucracy that these leaders would use to magnify their wealth and power.

What we see today is the result of generations of social evolution that has been controlled by such leadership. It is naïve to believe that our social structure is set up in a manner that is truly democratic, independent, or free. Rather, our society is a product of hundreds of years of politically motivated and selfish programs that were written and rewritten by generations of people with power and wealth. The vast majority of people are manipulated to believe that they are free, that their vote counts, and that they are of significance in the grander social plan.

The truth is that the people in power are nothing more than a clan of highly skilled puppeteers who know exactly how to create the world they desire, while giving the public just enough to feel free and significant. They control the media and propagandize society in a way that makes everything appear as though the common man's best interest is being kept in mind. They give good reasons for doing the things they do and create a box of safety within their reasoning to assure these beliefs continue. They can rape the economy of trillions of dollars in the name of safety, or simply approve themselves lavish pay raises and vacations by calling them business expenses, while the average person puts in a hard day's work, hoping to bring home enough money to pay his bills and feed his family.

While we tout our independence and democratic methods, most of us do not even realize that our society has evolved from a narrow directory of choices provided by these people, who not only currently hold power, but have held power for generations by virtue of family lineage, friends, and partnerships. While most people vote on issues that they believe are important, they often fail to realize that most of the issues, as well as the solutions, have actually been provided for them and not by them. When society has a complaint, the solutions invariably come from those in power. When society does not have a complaint, they create a problem and sick the media hounds on the public to provoke the will to change. They then create a solution that they believe will appease the public, but more importantly, will secure their wealth and power, and the wealth of those with whom they share a vested interest.

This illusion of democracy allows people to feel like they play a role in our country's development. However, more often than not, people vote on an issue only to wonder why nothing has changed, why they are not seeing the results that were promised, and why these people in power are not coming through for them. Leaders have weaseled their way around this for generations, but if we are ever to have true freedom, this must change.

Chapter 2
Evaluating Efficiency

When evaluating social efficiency, it is important to understand the relationship between people as individuals and within society as a whole. Each living human being is a member of society, no matter how they live, where they live or what they do for a living. Even social outcasts, hermits, and those who exhibit antisocial behavior, are still part of the functioning of society.

Like the functioning of a motor vehicle, every piece, including scraps and screws, contributes to the overall functioning of that system. If a piece weakens, breaks, or is taken away, the entire system is weakened unless the piece is replaced. This is a fairly simple concept called 'functionalism.' However, when we apply this to the laws of cause and effect, we can see that, as one piece weakens, another must work harder to compensate for the weakened piece. Allowing this to occur causes an imbalance and puts more stress on the other parts of the system, which then leads to other system failures and, eventually, a collapse of the entire system.

With this picture in mind, it becomes clear that to fully understand the efficiency of society, a person must first evaluate how efficient they are as an individual. Socrates said, "The unexamined life is not worth living." So, let us examine our lives.

I would like you to take a moment and ask yourself a few questions. I have narrowed this personal examination down to three crucial questions that will help you determine where you fit in the social order. Think deeply about each question and be completely honest with yourself as you answer. There is no right or wrong answer. This is simply an exercise for the purpose of personal discovery and self-awareness.

The first question everyone needs to answer about themselves concerns occupation or lack of occupation:

Do you absolutely love what you do and how you spend your day?

Whether your answer is yes or no, you must ask yourself the second and, arguably, the most important question of your life:

Do you feel *purpose* or personal *fulfillment* in what you do and how you spend your days?

The third and final question you must ask yourself is far less important on a personal level, but has been granted considerable importance in our current social system and the beliefs we have developed:

Do you feel that you are fairly compensated for the work you do?

There are not many people that can truthfully answer yes to any of these questions, and almost no one can answer yes to all three. This is extremely unfortunate considering that this means many people will spend their entire lives working in an occupation that they do not like, that does not give them a feeling of purpose, or for which they do not feel fairly compensated. We have evolved into a system where people often must choose between an occupation that is not personally fulfilling to them, but will bring them external material rewards, and an occupation that is internally rewarding, but does not offer fair compensation. This creates a perpetuation of negativity, because a job that has no internal reward must make up for it in material reward, while an occupation that does not offer a fair external reward, forces people to question the value of their internal rewards. Either way, the rewards, be they internal or external, become a very touchy matter.

In 2002, I met a high school English teacher who could answer yes to all of these questions except for the one concerning compensation. What made his story tragic was, as a single father of two, he was forced to give up the work he loved to do, and the fulfilling purpose he served, because he could not financially afford to teach. This man went back to school and eventually became an engineer.

Ironically, when I asked him the same three questions several years later, he answered no to all three of them. Today he goes to work as an engineer, he does what is required of him for the day, and he collects his paycheck. He no longer enjoys his work, his job is not personally fulfilling, and he still does not feel that he is compensated fairly. His answer to the third question was, "Considering the level of work I do, and the setback I took going back to school, I wouldn't exactly say the compensation is fair, but it is enough." This story is all too common under our current system, and the most unfortunate part is that the career a person has is their livelihood. Our careers consume a considerable amount of time in our lives and is a major identifying factor as to who we are. So if people do not feel purpose in their work, they will have difficulty finding purpose in their lives.

The good news is; this is not how it has to be. Things can be different, and by transforming some key aspects of our social system, people can be doing the work that they love to do. People can find purpose in their occupations, dedicate their lives to that purpose, and be happy. The most incredible part of the efficiency theory is that, by making a few significant adjustments, we will simultaneously assist people to achieve personal fulfillment and solve a multitude of other social problems. As society creates a system where people can spend their lives performing work that they enjoy, doing jobs that they are passionate about, and feeling fairly compensated, society as a whole will be happier, healthier, safer, and will run much more efficiently.

Relative Efficiency

Currently, the system in the United States is hindered by a phenomenon I call 'relative efficiency.' Essentially, this is where people will complete what is expected of them and nothing more. There are many people who go to work each day and finish what is required of them, period. Generally speaking, people do not show up to work and think about how much extra work they can do that day. The attitude is, "Why do more if I am not going to get paid for it?" The reason this happens is because the vast majority of people work in a profession that they are not passionate about. Many people are working jobs that have no personal meaning for them and no fulfilling effect on them. The primary reason they work in such jobs is to bring home a paycheck that will meet their financial needs. They often have no personal interest in the product that they are producing, as it was likely someone else's development and will often be sold or consumed by someone else.

What happens when people do not love what they do, when they do not feel purpose, fulfillment, or fair compensation? Most people will only perform up to the level of expectation. This means a person's efficiency will become relative to the task at hand or the requirement for the day. Some people may feel that they cannot relate to this phenomenon, and there are certainly people who go above and beyond simply because they are competitive or very driven individuals, but even these rare individuals are often ridiculed by others as over-achievers.

However, when you sit down with one of these people and find out how they truly feel, they still cannot answer yes to all three of those important questions, and, as a result, they will eventually get burned out from their efforts. Regardless of whether one accepts or denies this idea, be assured that this type of relative efficiency can be eliminated for good, or at least minimized, through a more efficient system.

Finding Efficiency

How can people discover what will make them individually more efficient? To discover what your most
efficient role is in the efficient society, you must look
deep within yourself and find something you are extremely passionate about. Passion for something is an
extremely powerful motive that drives us to perform.
Perhaps your passion is a hobby, or just something you
are really interested in. To seriously analyze this, look
away from this book and really think about the question in relation to yourself. Whatever you love to do so
much that you would do it whether you were paid for
it or not, your career should reflect this passion. When
you have found this passion, you need to ask yourself,
"If money was not an issue, and you could spend the
rest of your life studying, performing, teaching, selling,
advising, or sharing this passion, how different would
your life be?"

This passion is your life's social purpose. This is
where you will find personal fulfillment in the work
you do and in the way you spend each day of your
life.[10] Most importantly, this is where you will become
a major contributor to the overall efficiency of society.
This is where you become a solid piece of the perfectly
running engine. When all people are contributing in
such a manner, our personal efficiency, as well as our
efficiency as a social whole, will expand exponentially.
People will begin to see how each other person's individual passion relates to their own, and this will create
a feeling of unity as people begin to appreciate how
each other's passions contribute to the efficiency of the
social whole.

Society will become a synchronized web of the most powerful 'supercomputers' available: a human brain filled will purpose and passion. Rather than placing value on a certain step of production, we will place a fair value on each of the components necessary for its production. People will begin to realize that society cannot function without the roles that every person plays; just as a computer cannot function without the hardware, the processor, the programs, or the electricity to make it run.

With everyone contributing to society in such a manner, achievements will no longer be measured by what a single person does, but by what humanity has accomplished together. Value will not be placed on the man who invented the light bulb, but rather on the fact that working together, we created free energy. Ideals will no longer be centered on what one person can get out of the other. Instead, ideals will value the fact that together we freed the world of toxic pollution by inventing a way to effectively reuse our waste. People will pursue such accomplishments not for the power and profits they might gain as an individual, but for how their life's purpose could play a role in producing an accomplishment that benefits humanity. This notion in itself is awe-inspiring, but there is more to it than just doing the things we are passionate about. We need to get to the point where all members of society can appreciate each other.

Motivation and Manipulation

There are various types of motivational and manipulative forces we deal with every moment of our
lives. Some of these forces touch us in a direct manner
and others touch us indirectly or passively. Let me clar-
ify what I mean when I say direct or indirect manipulation: Direct manipulation is a form of manipulation
that is straightforward, easily defined, severely conse-
quential, and often the result of some outside physical
source. For example, fear is a form of direct manipulation. If a man has a gun pointed at him and he is told to
do something, out of fear, he will likely do whatever the
gun wielder asks. Fear is the manipulating factor, and
the gun is the source that produces the fear through
threat of physical harm, psychological stress, or danger
to his family if he does not comply. This is a very strong
form of direct motivation or manipulation.

An indirect motivator is one that is not as severe,
but has power due to the emotional or psychological
impact it produces. This type of manipulator does not
necessarily reach our internal survival threshold, but
attacks us in our psychological will and desires. An example of this would be money. Money is not essential
for life per se, but is strongly desired for its emotional
and psychological benefits. You would not die without
money. After all, the human species survived hundreds
of thousands of years before a monetary system was
ever developed. However, the fact that money can get
us so many things so easily, and that we are bombarded
by advertisements telling us what we supposedly can-

not live without, stimulates the natural greed we have as humans and contributes to the manipulative power money has over us.

Now that we understand how these various degrees of manipulation occur, let us look at some common motivators in all of our lives. The human psyche has been studied for centuries with an attempt to discover what motivates people. Kings and dictators of the past, along with employers, educators, and business owners of today, are only a few of the groups that have spent a great deal of time and money studying the factors that motivate people to perform and act a certain way. One reason for these studies is because some believe they can improve society through a vast implementation of motivational strategies that will influence people to get things done. However, on the darker side of these studies, we find the intention to control and manipulate people to behave in a manner that benefits those who are producing the motivators.

Motivational manipulation can range from something as obvious as paying someone to perform a certain act, to something as elusive as a subliminal message. These manipulative motivators are around us everywhere. Shopping malls, for example, are full of subtle stimuli that store managers have provided in order to stimulate a desired response in people. There are sounds and colors set up specifically to excite the hypothalamus gland. This gland then releases chemicals in the brain called endorphins, which will lighten a person's mood and allow sales representatives to have more influence over their buying behavior. These endorphins (dopamine in particular) are the same chemicals that are released in a euphoric, drug-induced state. This is why some people can easily become addicted to shopping, and why this strategy is effective in manipulating people.[11]

There are many other stimuli that people may, or may not, be aware of that influence us subconsciously. The temperature in a building, the odors we smell, and the placement of products, are all factors that are calculated for effective influence on the consumer. For example, as you walk through a grocery store, it is no accident that the most expensive and sweetest tasting cereals are placed at the eye-level of children, while the healthier cereals that appeal more to adults are placed on the upper shelves where the average-height adult can easily see them. These items are strategically placed in areas that will provide a stimulus for the targeted clients to create a desired response. Many people are aware of this and consider it no big deal, but the fact is, this is still a form of manipulation.[12]

These manipulations are not confined to consumer shopping. People are also under a great deal of manipulation when it comes careers. In each profession, administrators, managers, and business owners provide several forms of response mechanisms that are designed to manipulate what you do and how you feel about it.

During my undergraduate studies, I changed my major six times. Like many other people I have talked with, I was stuck in an ambivalent mental battle between emotion and logic. The question I continually asked myself was, "Do I want to spend the rest of my life doing something that I am truly passionate about, but will not provide a desired income? Or, should I major in something that will make me a lot of money, but that I really won't enjoy."

As I went through each stint in a particular field of study, I began interviewing people in those professions to determine if this was something I would be willing to do. I wanted to know if my new career choice would be worth sacrificing some loss of purpose in return for compensating material greed or vice versa. Through my interviews, I found that every profession was very similar in two respects, people felt overworked, and people felt controlled by some outside source, most commonly, money.

Money is, arguably, the single most influential factor in manipulating people under our current social system. People who are extremely wealthy have a lot of power and a lot of influence. No one can argue the influential power of money. This is essentially how the television show, *Fear Factor,* got started. Fear is considered by many to be the greatest direct manipulator and is far more effective at controlling people than money could ever be. This is proven daily in armed robbery cases, where people give up their money without hesitation when faced with the fear of death. Ironically, to demonstrate the influential power of money, television has made a game out of the two manipulative motivators.[13]

Anyone who has ever watched *Fear Factor* has essentially seen a psychological test to see if passive influence can overcome direct influence. In an extreme situation such as death, direct influence will almost always win, but money is not too far behind. People are entertained by seeing others do ridiculous things while fighting their fears, so money is used to manipulate them to provide this entertainment. If this is hard to believe, then explain why someone would allow thousands of tarantulas or cockroaches to crawl on them for 60 seconds. Would someone do this for the fun of it? Of course not, but if fifty thousand dollars was offered for doing it, someone may try to face their fears to get the money.

After acknowledging the influential power of money, arguably, the second most powerful indirect influencing factor is guilt. On the guilt-ridden side of passive manipulation, the education profession provides a great example. Anyone who has worked, or been trained as, a professional educator has heard over and over again that educating is an incredibly noble profession. What they do not tell you is that every time a teacher addresses the taboo subject of salary, they are ridiculed and questioned about their motives for teaching. Ask any teacher how many times they have heard colleagues say, "I hope you aren't doing this for the money." Or, "If it's about the money, then you are in this profession for the wrong reason." Ironically, in most other professions, salary is a major motivational factor for choosing that occupation. Could you imagine entering law school or business school and hearing your colleagues or the professors say, "I hope you aren't doing this for the money?"

We must face the fact that money is an extremely manipulative factor in our lives. By allowing money to have such manipulative force, we are granting those people who have the most money, the most power. This causes some serious identity problems for a society that so badly wants to claim to be in pursuit of freedom and equality. If you are not the holder of the money, you have little power, and are one of the people being manipulated. Therefore, you are only as free as the people with the wealth allow you to be.

Wealth = Freedom

How many times have we come across an ad suggesting we can be independently wealthy, or that we can achieve financial freedom? They say this because people know that the more wealth you have, the more freedom you have. We see this demonstrated every second of the day all over the world. Take Hurricane Katrina, for example; those people who had the money to leave, left, and did not experience the suffering that many of the poorer people were forced to endure. There were some people who stayed out of denial or ignorance, but many of them simply did not have the money that would have granted them the freedom to leave. Think about it, if you are barely making ends meet, and you are not able to get credit, then it is pretty hard to say, "Alright kids! We're taking a trip up north to stay in a hotel for a few days." Quite the contrary, these people felt trapped.

Millions of other people experience this lack of freedom on a daily basis as well. One great thing about being involved in the public school system is that it has provided me the opportunity to get an in-depth understanding of people from various socio-economic statuses. Most schools are put into districts that require students within a neighborhood boundary to attend a school with in those boundaries. So it is very common to see a natural segregation of students based on their community's socio-economic status. I chose to change schools several years in a row because I wanted to see firsthand what different communities were like by interacting with them in a close environment. In doing so, I worked with students and families who ranged from millionaire status to poor and homeless and everything in between.

The most amazing difference I discovered was the level of freedom each group believed they had. This also resulted in enormous experience gaps between these varied groups. The wealthy had the freedom to travel and experience the world, to receive tutoring on difficult subjects, to eat where they chose, and to wear what they wanted. The wealthy seemed to radiate a sense of royalty about them. They not only expressed the freedom to do what they wanted, but projected the confidence that they had the right to do as they pleased and deserved only the best.

The poor on the other hand, rarely had any experience outside of their own community. Many had never been outside of the city they were from and certainly not outside of the state, or country. They often had to wear what was given to them and eat what was provided for them, rather than what they chose. These people had no money and, as a result, they felt stagnant and repressed. They did not have a sense of freedom, but rather, they felt controlled. This often led to a rebellious attitude, which unfortunately exacerbated the problem, as they often refused the help that was meant to improve their situation, such as education and training.

This is not a problem that only the poor experience. Many average U.S. Citizens do not have the financial freedom to travel to Europe, dine at exotic international restaurants, and experience the broader aspects of the world. Many people feel trapped when their car breaks down, because they cannot afford to drop a few hundred dollars to have it repaired. I am sure that every person reading this book, even the wealthy, can think of a time when they felt their freedom was hindered because of a financial obligation elsewhere. Maybe an investment was lost because the capital was not available at the time, or maybe a family member got sick and medical expenses had to be paid for out of a child's college fund. From whatever perspective we look at it, most people can relate to this experience in one way or another.

Once we get our system on track and our society is running with the efficiency we know is possible, these problems will be minimized, if not eliminated all together. Through a more efficiently run social system, our sense of freedom will be expanded exponentially, and our attitudes towards one another and the system we serve will be appreciated rather than despised.

Chapter 3
Walls of Inefficiency

The Greed Factor

The United States has become the greatest economic power in the history of the world by tapping into two of the strongest human motivators, greed and envy. Our country is built on the notion that, if I work hard enough, I can become as good as, or better than, the person next door. We have so much admiration for the people who have pulled themselves from the pits of poverty to become what our society considers wealthy and successful. We even share their stories as motivation for others, so that they will believe it is possible for them as well. This notion has been coined a dream, "The American Dream," that is supposed to be achievable by anyone in a land where even an impoverished person has the ability to literally go from rags to riches.

We claim that a person born at the bottom of society is not stuck at the bottom. All individuals have the opportunity to capitalize on multiple resources provided and lift themselves to any level of success that can be dreamt up. Though this is advertised as one of the greatest aspects of American society, this opportunity has also been used as a form of negative manipulation, where the likelihood of such success is advertised as something that most people can do. This relationship between the manipulative forces of money through greed and envy is pushed by the wealthy and the powerful so that everyone will believe that this can happen to them. Businesses and other agencies advertise and broadcast examples of the American Dream at its best to promote a continued desire for more wealth and more power, and all you have to do is work harder——for them (the business owners).

Many people have heard a story about a homeless youth that worked hard and became something extraordinary. I remember a story that my 5th grade teacher used to tell the class about a woman who started out washing dishes for a restaurant. She worked there for a long time and, because of her hard work, she eventually became the manager. After years of continued hard work, she eventually bought a restaurant of her own. The truth is, examples like this are extremely rare, and it is really a person's passion, mixed with a little luck and timing, that truly offers them the opportunity to get there. However, these stories motivate us, because we are taught that if one person did it, we can too.

Businesses use this stimulus to get people to work long and laborious hours by offering employees more money and a potential promotion. Businesses do this to people because it costs less than hiring another employee. Promised rewards also drive managers to push employees to work harder and longer. Companies offer financial incentives to managers who perform above average by driving their employees to high levels of stress, and feeding their greed for more money.[14] When this form of motivation no longer works, they turn to our strongest motivator, fear. The might warn, "You will lose your job if you do not meet this standard or quota." They get people to *voluntarily* work 60 to 80 hours a week doing something they do not like to do—to ensure that they are seen as an asset to the company—because they need the money and do not want to lose their jobs.

I spent some time working for a company in the fitness industry that sold personal training to club members. They would use the very same sales tactics to persuade to people to buy training that they did to manipulate their sales people to work harder and longer hours. They would tell them, "It is simple and easily achievable. You just need to do what you are told to do. You will be promoted very quickly and be making a six-figure income in no time." They very cleverly designed the job structure so that every position was called a director, manager, or manager in training. They would repetitively tell every potential new-hire that it was simple and that they would move up very quickly.

This was the only sales position I had ever worked, and I quit after a very short time, because of what I considered unethical practices. Sales people were trained to lie to members about the prices in an attempt to get them to pay more. They would focus all efforts on closing the deal, and treat them well until their three-day grace period was over. They would purposely use fancy jargon that members wouldn't understand, and then use their inability to understand as a reason why they need help. They consistently used the classic bait-and-switch method of sales, and when sales we low, they would even lead people to believe that without purchasing training, they would likely get hurt or even lose years off of their lives.

While I was there, I was constantly running into people who had worked for this company and I would interview them at every chance I got on why they no longer worked for the company. What I found was that the turnover rate was enormous, even in the management positions, because employees rarely reached the potential that they were told they would reach. The sales people were sick of having to lie to customers just to get sales, and the managers were sick of having to pressure their sales people to perform for unfair compensation, just so they could get their managerial pay.

We have all seen how powerful money is in manipulating us. People often choose their life's work based on the amount of money it will bring them. People will even work completely meaningless jobs as long as it will provide for their monetary desires. This motive comes in the form of desire and is presented to all of us as a goal for everyone. The desire is strong and the goal is simple: that maybe you too can become as rich and powerful as the people society has trained us to admire. Just like the many people who have experienced the same thing I did when I accepted the job selling training, we are taught that it is easy to achieve, as long as we do what we are told.

The Capitalist Paradox

If sales and commission jobs are at one end of the spectrum, then salaries are at the other. A salaried position is the Capitalist Paradox. A salary is the first socialist concept accepted in a capitalist society.[15] Salaries provide jobs where, no matter how much work is done, the employee will receive a designated amount of money. Today, a large number of the jobs in America have become salaried positions and people enjoy the certainty a salary provides. Salaries are often adjusted, and even related to an hourly-pay equivalent, but they are a solidified form of compensation nonetheless. Sometimes people are offered bonuses, or commission incentives, on top of their salary to provide further motivation, but, for the most part, a salary is set to provide a secure and predictable amount of money.

Salaries are not a bad idea. In fact, salaries are one of the best forms of compensation in our current social system. However, the problem with salaries has always been balancing the amount of work expected for a given salary. While salaries can be nice, unless a person is passionate about their work they will rarely work up to their full potential. This is directly related to relative efficiency. How often does a salaried person do just enough work required for the day and go home? That is not to say that people on salary do not work hard. Many salaried jobs require an extraordinary amount of work, even massive amounts of overtime, but that is what is written in the job contract. The question is, how often do people go above and beyond what is required to succeed at the salaried job simply because they love what they do?

The fact is, people rarely go above and beyond the call of duty unless there is a reward for it, and if the reward is not internal, a salary is not going to push them to perform.[16] This is a key reason why societies find it difficult to raise the efficiency of their economic systems. Not only does this create a problem of productive inefficiency, it also creates a problem in the individual's psychosocial efficiency when people are unable to find purpose and internal reward in their productivity.

Here is where the salaried position is fundamentally flawed, monetary rewards reach their motivational limits, and our social efficiency crumbles.[17] The belief that money is the answer is not something that is internally suggested. This idea has been inculcated by centuries of manipulating human desires through greed and envy, using media, education, advertising, and propaganda.

The only way to break this trance that has been bestowed upon us is through fundamental changes in key aspects of our social and economic systems. Once the systems have been altered, this will ultimately lead to a change in belief. Once this change in belief has occurred, people will experience a tremendous sense of freedom, security and happiness. We will feel freed from an ideology that the elite have meticulously planted into the social mentality. We will feel free to work the jobs we love and to enjoy how we spend our days.

Better yet, we will be freed from the political prodding that has shaped our society into its current state of inefficiency.

Capitalism is a wonderful theory, but, in its purest form, it causes many problems. It creates severe and vast social imbalances, and carries our whole economy on a continuous swinging pendulum. We are currently in the midst of the greatest economic crisis since the great depression, and this was seeded by the greed which capitalism creates. In my relatively short time on this earth, I have already experienced two "recessions." There are some living people, my grandparents included, who were alive during the great depression, and are now again facing the worst economic trouble since that time. It seems that every decade comes with new challenges and nationwide financial troubles. Over the last century, our country has repeatedly been on the verge of economic collapse. This is due to the fact that we have been trained to be greedy, to seek greatest financial reward for the least amount of work possible, and don't worry about any internal purpose.

Competition

Competition can have both positive and negative effects on society. In this chapter, we will discuss the problems it causes and how an Efficient Society will use competition only for its positive effects.

The competitive seeds planted by the market economy are certainly responsible for some of the most profound accomplishments of our time. During World

War II, there was a world-wide competition to develop the most powerful weapon known to man. This resulted in nuclear energy. By making life into a competitive game, businesses and individuals are stimulated to constantly invent new technologies and improve on others. This is seen as a means to becoming the next rich and powerful person. The notion is simple: By providing a product better than the others, people will prefer to buy the better product. This will shift wealth to the maker of the better product. Again, wealth is the ultimate motive, and a continuous expansion of improved products is the result. This type of competition extrapolates through time and leads to better and better products.

Think back to the laws of cause and effect. Here, a connection can be established between the cause, *people competing*, and the effect, *an improved product*. The question is, which is actually the cause, and which is the effect? Are people instinctively competitive, which creates a desire to invent a better product, regardless of the benefit to the business? Or, is it the businesses asking them to create a better product to gain the edge in sales? Regardless of whether the chicken or the egg came first, the point is that competition is the fuel for growth and there is a strong concern that, without this competition, growth could slow greatly or even halt altogether.

While competition has its benefits, there are also some negative social consequences arising from such competitive attitudes. The competitive spirit has been the prime force in capitalist society since its inception.

Many people in strong capitalist societies have never experienced any other way of living. This has contributed to generations of people who have developed this ideology that competition is necessary, but it has also reached some extremes. From designer clothing to plastic surgery, from jewelry to exotic cars, and from real estate to personal experiences, everything in life has become a competition. There are some people who have realized this is an impossible way to live and have given up on the social competition.[18] There are others who strive for the unattainable victory as though it were a life or death competition. These are the people who are of the greatest concern for the Efficiency Theory.

Everywhere we look today, people are competing over the most ridiculous and miniscule things. Competition is no longer a game played on a field or a product of Darwin's evolutionary ideas. Competition has become a way of life that consumes us in every aspect of our lives. Competition is not isolated to materialistic ownership of goods; it has become a massive challenge within our psychological and social fabrics as well.

Growing up, I can remember participating in the family gift exchange at Christmas time. This joyous time always ended up in a competition when one family member bought a better Christmas gift than the others. Multiple implications proceed from such a practice. First is the materialistic part of the competition: Whoever gives the best gift shows that they have the most money and are better than the others. Then comes the psychological competition: Is it really necessary to out-do everyone else? What are these people trying to prove? Finally comes the social competition: The status level for the person who gave the better gift is now higher, or so it is perceived to be.

What most people do not look at is the cause and effect relationship within these acts. This often resulted in negative comments about the giving family member, based on speculations about their motives for giving a particular gift. This is not isolated to my family. Every person I know has had some type experience like this, whether it is the neighbor who bought a new car to outdo the person living down the street, the person who must flaunt their designer bags and clothing, or the person at the staff party who feels the urge to one-up every other person in the room with a story of their own.

People's lives become consumed with competition and getting the upper hand. Another result of this competitive atmosphere is the everlasting and continuous negative feelings that are created by these people. An even greater concern is the message that is passed from these people to the others: That whether they like it or not, they are playing the game. More often than not, whether a person wants to be in this competitive game or not, they feel compelled to become a part. These people stir up emotions in unsuspecting people and, in this way, stimulate the drive to compete. This is harmful to us as people and as a social whole because it creates friction and wastes energy that can be used elsewhere.

The competitive phenomenon in this form has many harmful effects on individuals and on society as a whole because of the effect it has on each individual.

People do become consumed by this ideology. These competitions become the foundation of their lives and ultimately lead to one of the greatest contributing factors to our social inefficiency, the battle between purpose and desire. A person caught up in the competitive mind-set will indubitably give up meaning and purpose in life for a career they dislike, as long as it earns a lot of money, because they become obsessed with trying to keep up. These people substitute their true life's purpose for a counterfeit purpose, a purpose that has been imposed on them by a manipulative game of competition. Their life's purpose is to win a competition that only exists in their minds. What they do not realize is that this is a competition that could never end, and ultimately cannot be won, because of its extreme relativity—relativity that is, and always will be, base on perception.

Why We Are Currently So Inefficient

We have established that society has been shaped around a monetary reward system rather than a more purposeful and fulfilling reward system. There are millions of people who do not care what they are doing as long as they are making a lot of money. There are millions more who will make the same amount of money regardless of what they do, so they do just enough to get by. There are some computer technicians who waste several hours a day at work, playing video games because they can, and they know they will still get paid. Who has not seen people at work who sit at their desks and talk to their friends on the telephone for hours, because they can and they will still get paid? These people have skills that are either not being used or are being completely wasted on useless activity.[19]

This is fine under the current system because these people are achieving the single most important objective they have created for their lives, making money. A major cause of our social decline is the fact that money rules people's personal, social, and life-long objectives. People are more concerned with making money than saving lives. People have been trained to believe they will be happier with wealth than with purpose, but it does not have to be this way.

Let us now look even deeper into the reasons for social inefficiency. The degree of efficiency is relative to our behavior as a working group. If a person's behavior at work is to talk on the phone to a friend instead of working on a task, then it is the behavior that is our concern. This means it is important to understand why people behave the way they do. Behaviors are a product of a person's beliefs. A perfect example of this is the suicide bombings the world has dealt with for years. What could convince a man to kill himself and hundreds of others? Perhaps communion with God, and the ownership of several virgins in the afterlife, would do it. In the mind of a Christian or an atheist, this sounds ridiculous, but all of us do things every day because of a belief we hold that others, who do not hold that belief, may think is strange.

The beliefs we hold are what control our behaviors. Whether it is a superstition, a religion, a belief in a person, an event, a commercial, or a theory, we all act the way we do because of how we believe. However, when these beliefs are not understood by others, it is because they are not shared by them. Those people who share the belief that these men will go to heaven for these acts, do understand why they are doing it, and support them in their actions.

Beliefs are also extremely complicated, because beliefs come to people through a filter of their own perception. This perception is either constructed through experiences or through teachings. When people lack the experiences needed to develop their own beliefs, they rely on what they have been taught. This creates an extreme problem that I will touch on briefly here. It must be understood that teaching in all forms is fallible in many respects and a significant way of manipulating people and their beliefs. This is not to say that all forms of teaching and manipulation are bad, it is just wise to be aware of these forces at work.

The Effects of Perception

The reason teaching is so fallible is because the nature of teaching is conceptually and perceptually biased. It starts with a concept, such as, "Dogs are nice." This is a belief of the teacher, because the teacher was taught this and validated the belief through her own experiences with dogs. Therefore, to her, dogs have always been nice. However, this very concept can be taught to another person and, when they take this belief to the wrong dog, they get bitten. This person may then become a teacher who promotes the concept that dogs are mean, vicious animals. With this example, it can be seen that when a concept is taught, it is taught in terms of the teacher's beliefs. These beliefs have formed through the teacher's experiences or been passed to them through teachers they have encountered, in an enormous chain of perceptual filters. Whether the concepts taught are objective facts or not is a matter of philosophy.

However, it is important to understand that any concept being shared is interpreted through an individual filter and expressed as a belief. That belief is then taught to others, where it then becomes their belief as well. Since many people do not have the freedom, or capability, to test the new belief through an experiential realm, they simply accept it as true. The terrorists who do suicide bombings do not believe they will commune with God because they have experienced this. They believe it because they have been taught to believe it.

For the Efficiency Theory to make sense, people must realize that the beliefs they hold have either been taught to them by others or have been based on personal experience through their own perceptions. Many U.S. citizens believe that this country has created the best social system in history. Americans have been taught to believe this by those who are rich and have experienced this. The media, business, and teachers affirm this belief by showing examples of how bad life is in countries that do not use our system. People who have traveled extensively can share their experiences, of how our system provides much greater rewards to its people than any other system they have seen. However, we must remember that such pronouncements usually come through the speaker's perceptual filter as a wealthy, first world citizen.[20]

We all live in our own worlds. On a physical level, people share a large common place. However, within this physical world each person also has their own individual consciousness, which gives them a perception of living in their own world. People often get caught up in their individual worlds and forget what is happening around them, until something, or perhaps some person, does something that affects their world. This creates a new awareness and forces people to make a decision about that new world they both now share. The choices are to either ignore this new awareness or accommodate it. Unfortunately, people often choose to ignore each other because it takes less effort or because they simply do not want to change. This is a dangerous route to take, because these two worlds will eventually have to accommodate each other and many others also. The best choice, then, would be to accommodate each other's perceptions in this new combined world. However, to successfully blend their perceptual worlds into one, whatever they decide must be mutual. If the blend is not mutually considered, then the worlds are not blended, but rather, one world has taken over the other.

As for an example of this, I will share my observation of a guy at the local pub. I watched a man at a pub literally bump into almost every girl he saw throughout the evening. He was intentionally attempting to converge his world with each girl's world, hoping that he would find one to accommodate his world. Once he finds a girl that will accommodate his world, they will either begin a mutual blending of the two worlds, or one of the two worlds will take the other over. This blending of two worlds starts out as a very brief blend, but over time can develop into a successful and long-term blend. However, it is very important to realize that these two worlds will never really become one. Rather they will be two separate worlds that permanently overlap, and if only one of them puts forth the energy to coexist, both of their overlapping worlds will collapse.

In a marriage, the husband and wife do not become the same person; they simply share a larger world in which their two worlds overlap. We call these overlapping world's families. On a grander scale, we call them communities, then cities, states, countries and so on. In these community worlds, people agree to share their individual worlds and remain together within the larger world. People choose to make decisions, accommodations, and contributions according to the community's needs and desires. People have families, friends, colleagues, and acquaintances within their overlapping community worlds, but these are the simple examples of overlaps that most people are aware of. There are still billions of other worlds around us that we may never directly come in contact with, and there are billions of overlapping community worlds that we also may never become directly aware of.

However, to live in a harmonious and efficient world, it is extremely important to realize that each of these personal and community worlds, create a web of overlapping perceptual worlds that are interrelated to the grander physical world. Whether people realize it or not, they are in a forced marriage to every other person on this planet, because we share this globe as a common home. Though many people may not be consciously aware of this overlap, it is a key understanding that must be awakened in order to achieve social efficiency and personal happiness. It is absolutely imperative that more people realize this if we are to become an efficient society.

A Lesson from the Ancient Ones

What the mainstream does not spend much time teaching is that some of the most harmonious and prosperous civilizations were actually from ancient times, from times so long ago that we struggle to grasp what life was like then and how such societies functioned. These civilizations were built on fairness and trade rather than greed and envy. These civilizations had the efficiency to create social structures that are difficult for us to comprehend today. During this time, people focused on the whole, rather than the individual, and the prosperity of their civilizations was measured in millenniums, rather than in centuries or decades.

The ancient Egyptians were, arguably, one of the most efficient and amazing civilizations ever known. So why haven't we tried to emulate more pieces of their society? Around the turn of the century, Egyptologists discovered an ancient tablet that contained some insight into their way of life. Dating back to the times when the pyramids were built, the Egyptians had a mathematical formula for dividing things in such a proportionate way that virtually anything could be distributed evenly among any number of people.[21] In this particular tablet, they explained a way of dividing nine loaves of bread such that fifteen people could have exactly the same amount. Most people wouldn't care as long as it looked close, but these ancient people would make sure the shares were equal, even though they had to make several more cuts in the bread. Now that is efficiency. There is something to a society that built a structure that still marvels us today, and it is no coincidence that this society found efficiency in its equality.

The time has come for people to wake up and realize that current society is far less efficient than our predecessors. We have become so obsessed with what we believe we need to be happy, what people have told us we need to be happy, and what society tells us is necessary for happiness, that we struggle to see that the answer is really quite simple. If the people of this world want to achieve true happiness in their lifetime, things must change. Such changes can only begin through a change in perception (a product of education and experience), because perception influences our beliefs, and beliefs ultimately determine behaviors.

The Evolution and Effects of Selfishness

Selfishness is an inherent biological imperative that has been evolving since the beginning time. Evolution has required people to take care of themselves to survive. Survival of the fittest meant looking out for number one and doing whatever it takes to eliminate the competition. This was crucial for survival, because he who did not have the resources, wealth, or physical strength to live, became weak and died. Generation after generation, we have taught each other that we need to learn to take care of ourselves. People are given a vision of success, and they are taught they can reach this dream by working hard, manipulating the right people, and leaving behind that lower class of people they once were. Because of this philosophy, people have become so self-involved and concerned with what will make their own personal lives better that they often forget, neglect, and even take from other people all around them.

When we step back and really look at this for what it is, we begin to see life as an elaborate game. The problem with this perspective is that games are played with the intent to win and, where there is a winner, there is always a loser. Many people who play life as a game take pride in their ability to manipulate and destroy another person's world in order to justify and provide for their own personal world, sometimes without even realizing the broader effect their personal victory creates. People fail to realize that everyone on this planet is interconnected at the physical and social levels, in one way or another, and, as a result, they fail to take responsibility for the fact that, if we are not contributing to the solution, we contributing to the problem.

As people spend more time in their personal mental worlds, they become more selfish and less inclined to see the grander scheme of life. By focusing on themselves and their selfish goals, they begin to justify their beliefs and actions tediously. Once they begin to justify, they have separated themselves from others and attempted to construct a social wall. Since everything one person does in their personal world affects all other people in one way or another, these walls result in a perpetual deterioration of society. Due to the cause and effect relationship of these actions, the failure to acknowledge this fact and act accordingly, contributes further to the social problems we have today.

To illustrate this idea, imagine flying on an airplane. Prior to 1999 smoking was allowed on many airline flights. This was to suit those individual worlds that desired to smoke, mostly the upper-class Americans and British. Over time, people realized that the actions of a single cigarette smoker on the airplane negatively affected hundreds of people around them, whether they were a smoker or not. Thus the phrase, "second hand smoke," was coined. If only one person on a flight chose to smoke a cigarette, all 200 people on the flight were subjected to the odor, the tar, and any other negative side-effects from the smoke.[22] The community world of the airplane contained hundreds of overlapping individual worlds, which were affected by as few as one smoker. In response to this emerging insight, the airline industry was forced to acknowledge the other people on the flight and respect their personal worlds as well. This realization eventually led to a banning of smoking on all flights because of the cancerous effects one person's action, in their personal world, had on another person in the grander world. Storytellers call this notion cause and effect; physicists call it the Second Law of Thermodynamics: action-reaction. It has also been called the 'Ripple Effect' and the 'Butterfly Effect.' Regardless of the name it is given, the facts are undeniable. Everything a person does in their personal world will affect the grander all-encompassing world of the whole.

When closely observing the laws of cause and effect and its association with thermodynamics, the property of balance becomes a key issue. This is not just a natural phenomenon in the physical world, but a psychosocial phenomenon as well. The natural laws show that any action will be balanced by creating an equal and opposite reaction. Balance appears to be nature's objective. This phenomenon is much easier to see in the physical world. For example, if a person hits an impenetrable wall, the same amount of force generated, will be pushed back into the fist. If a forest becomes overgrown with trees, it becomes more susceptible to fire and disease, which will ultimately balance the growth by killing off the weaker trees. As the planet become over-populated, our negative effects create more and more natural disasters that cause calamity.

People can observe this balancing force in society as well. For every action an individual takes in society, an equal and opposite social reaction occurs. This could be a physical action, a verbal action, a business action, or any other significant or insignificant action. By looking closer at the balancing factors in society, it becomes clear that all people and their actions are interconnected with the entire world society. For example, for every rich man there is a poor man, or multiple poor men, and for every giver there is a taker. Balance is nature's objective and since society is an aspect of nature, it needs to be balanced as well. Unfortunately, the current social system can only achieve balance through a pendulum of positive and negative events. The secret of social efficiency is to minimize the pendulum's swing, and achieve balance before the pendulum ever starts to swing.

Social Cause and Effect

Imagine ten friends have pooled their money together and bought a winning lotto ticket. At pay out, the ten receive one million dollars. A harmonious and balanced reaction to this would be that every person receives $100,000. However, if one person decides that they deserve a higher percentage than the others, they are no longer balanced and chaos will occur. People who take more do so at the expense of another. This happens because people do not evaluate or accept the social cause and effect their world has on others. Instead we think about the big screen television that all of the commercial tell us we can not live with out. This provokes greed, which ultimately results in disharmony.

As people's private worlds consume them through selfishness and greed, they lose sight of the objective and the result is inefficiency. In this example, the goal was to win the lotto and the goal was achieved. Is it really necessary to fight for $110,000 of the split rather than the agreed $100,000? Is it worth the chaos, the heartache, the lawsuits, and the loss of friendship? To achieve and retain peace and harmony, balance must be accomplished ahead of time and then maintained. People must focus on the overall goal as a whole and stop focusing on themselves. Most people have a common goal, to live a comfortable life and contribute to the evolution of man. If this were not the case, then death would be the ultimate pursuit of man.

The lottery is a very light example, but the demonstrated effects are very real. Let us now look into some more common and very serious aspects of society. It is important to understand that as the highest corporate salaries rise, they do so at the expense of someone else; either low-level jobs are cut, blue-collar salaries are lowered, the consumer is charged more, or jobs are shipped overseas for cheaper labor. Any way you look at it, someone must take a loss for another person to gain. There is the possibility that profits rose and all workers will receive raises, but even that has a cause and effect relationship. Perhaps the rise in profits was the result of business-A paying lower amounts of money to its suppliers or business-B. This would then force the supplying company (business-B) to cut profits or over-charge someone else later. Whatever the cause may be, inevitably, the effect is that someone else is losing.

Some people may argue that this is okay, on the theory that this provides the balancing factor in the market. However, what most people fail to see is the effect that this "swinging pendulum" scenario has on society. Consider again the laws of cause and effect. As business-A gains, business-B loses, but more importantly is the effect this has on society as a whole. Since business involves people, it has an enormous influence on society. Rather than balancing business-B's job losses by creating new positions in business-A, often the reality is that the CEOs and managers will receive hefty bonuses and absorb a good percentage of any gains. This is typically how business is run. The fate of all employees is in the hands of a few people at the top, who tend to be completely out of touch with the average worker. This not only leads to economic imbalance, but also to an imbalance in society as a whole.

What we see as a result of cause and effect, is that society will eventually attempt to find equilibrium through various criminal activities. Using the bonus example, we can see that, while a few at the top benefit greatly, most people will not, and others will actually suffer because of it. This will result in more poor people on the street, more people motivated to steal to survive, and more people motivated to act out in violence due to anger and bitterness about their unfortunate position in the world. Whether it be by auto theft, robbery, or because the CEO must spend extra money to equip everything he owns with elaborate alarm systems, society will attempt to find balance. Cause and effect demonstrates that, be*cause* some people lost in the wake of another person's gain, the *effect* will come as people turn to other ways of providing for their needs and desires. This is where balance is ultimately attained. So if CEOs want to play the self-righteous card and claim they deserve the bonuses and criminals are just bad people, they need to think again and realize that they are major contributors to the problem.

People find their sanctuary in blame. When crime occurs, most people will place blame on the thief and never look at how they are personally affecting society. Flaunting our lavish cars and showing the poor how much they are missing out on has an extreme effect on people and society. Many people started seeing this first hand, as the U.S. economic system began to crumble in early 2008. While millions of people were losing their jobs, getting pay cuts, and losing their homes, major corporations, including banking CEOs that contributed to the problem, were receiving multi-million-dollar bonuses. Rather than taking those hundreds of billions of dollars and creating more jobs, the money went to just a few people at the top.

The law of cause and effect shows that their greed effected thousands of jobs that could have been retained by the money that went to their bonuses, ultimately resulting in more problems, more crime, and a tainted economic system. In 2008, CBS News reported that $14 billion of the government "bailout" money, was paid to investment banking CEOs. Simple math shows that the government could have created 280,000 jobs with salaries of $50,000 with that $14 billion dollars. These CEO's imprudent management is what lead to the economic decline, yet they given enormous bonuses (above their already enormous salaries) at the expense of 280,000 above average paying jobs.

Isn't it interesting that when wealth is taken or denied at the corporate level, it is called "good business," but when it is taken at the personal level, it is considered "theft?" To achieve efficiency, we need to eliminate this terrible cycle altogether and create balance from the start. When balance is achieved in the beginning, these negative reactions will no longer occur.

Under our current system, balancing the economic pendulum is only possible through positive and negative consequences and action-reaction relationships. In fact, the current system not only thrives on this imbalance, but teaches it's members that this is the best way. This is why there are so many social problems under this system. The only way to eliminate these imbalances, to reduce the crimes that are fueled primarily by desperation, jealousy, greed, envy, and to achieve happiness for all people in their individual and community worlds, is to create a balanced, more efficient social system. The efficient community and the individuals involved in this system will all work together towards a common goal, and balance will be achieved through purpose, fairness, oneness, and the appreciation of all.

Chapter 4
The Need for Change

Rewiring Beliefs

As I described in the previous chapter, many of the beliefs people have are the reasons for their greed and envy. Manipulative forces have been used for centuries to teach society to believe in a way that causes these behaviors. The first step towards achieving social efficiency is rewiring our beliefs: but how can we change a belief that has been engrained so deeply, a belief that has been validated every minute of every day, and still is, when we see some people with so much material wealth?

The only way to truly eliminate greed is to eliminate envy by changing our perception. This is again a cause-and-effect relationship. Envy is created when people compare what others have to what they have. When people see that other people have things that they do not, and that they desire, envy is manifested. People who have the things they want, and the things they believe they need, are rarely envious of others. Even if other people have great things, if it is not something that is personally desired by another, then envy ceases to exist. For example, a person may love dogs and have an extremely rare dog worth a million of dollars. Most other people will not be envious of the dog unless they too are collectors of rare dogs. Instead, the envy is in the *idea* of the wealth this person possesses, as demonstrated by the purchase of such a dog.

This example demonstrates the relativity of greed because people have many different tastes, desires, and needs. The epitome of envy is created when television shows the movie star who owns an entire island in the Caribbean, or the basketball star who owns a massive collection of exotic cars. The envy comes from this ability to gloat, when those people who have so much wealth appear to recklessly throw money around, as if life were a game of monopoly, while the majority struggles to pay their personal bills. This is a constant reminder that some people are the haves and others are the have-nots. This display of unnecessary spending is what creates envy. If this were eliminated, or at least moderated, envy would equally be eliminated or moderated.[23]

This is not to say people have no right to desire an exotic car, however gluttony should be put aside. Perhaps owning one exotic car would be nice and, if a person decides they want another, they can spend some time saving for it, or trade in the one they have.

An Efficient Society where greed and envy would be minimal would be based on equality, not equality in the sense that everyone is the same, but in the sense that everyone has an equal chance of achieving the same level of prosperity. This requires closing the enormous gap in wealth that puts prosperity so far out of reach for most people. Such a society does not have a ruling class, nor is there poverty. In this society, everyone is the ruling class. Whether a person cleans the streets or builds rockets, they are recognized for their contribution to society, and they are compensated fairly for it.

Today there is a new essence that surrounds the world. This is due to the nature of globalization and to rapid advancements in technology, which are catapulting human psychological and sociological evolution. In the summer of 2005, scientists from the University of Chicago published a discovery that not only is the human brain still evolving, but in the last several thousands of year it has been evolving at an increasingly rapid pace.[7]

Historically, we can look at the landmark ages, the Ancient World, the Middle Ages, the Renaissance, the Industrial Revolution, and the technological revolution. As we look at history, it can be seen that the further back we go, the slower and less significant the changes were. Where it took tens of thousands of years to progress from using stones for tools to using metals for tools, it took only decades to go from cars, to airplanes, to space travel, and beyond. As time has progressed, the dawn of each age has come at shorter intervals, and the advances have become exponentially more extreme. As these major changes occur, our social norms are required to make major adjustments. People are forced to re-evaluate their beliefs based on new findings and people begin to see life in a new light.

Today technological advancements are occurring so rapidly that our brains struggle to keep up. Currently, society is faced with issues such as cloning, space travel, stem cell research, alternative energy, and artificial intelligence, but our social policies, laws, and many of our beliefs are still structured around issues from tens, hundreds, and even thousands of years ago. This is causing our social and psychological structures to spin out of control. In light of these new findings, society is forced to change and people to re-evaluate their beliefs, just as people had to do when they discovered that the world was not flat. Based on new findings, people develop new ideas, new desires, and new philosophies as to what is important in life, and they adjust their beliefs and social structures accordingly.[24] Our current social structure is outdated and our policies need a tune-up if we are to successfully integrate our lives with this unprecedented growth.

To effectively accommodate these advances, we need to increase our efficiency. An efficient system is one that uses all of its resources with minimal waste. This means goals will be achieved much more rapidly and more time is left for personal use. Since everyone is working, all of our financial needs will be taken care of and greed and envy will be eliminated, leaving society with a feeling of fairness and togetherness. This will rapidly diminish the negativity associated with greed and envy. Instead, people will come together as a whole, working towards a common goal. They will realize that the most important thing is to experience life to its fullest and not to work it away trying to win a superimposed competition that means nothing.

Greed and Politics

The main objective we should have as a society is to achieve *ultimate efficiency*, but people will never understand this if they have not experienced it. Efficiency is the goal surrounding most major growth and is the basis for all advancement. The tools, medicines, and technologies society has developed are rapidly becoming more and more efficient, but our social structure has stayed relatively stagnant. The cause of this stagnation in our social advancement is found in the continuous political battles and in the large number of treacherous quick fixes politicians have come up with to appease the public.

A more specific reason our efficiency is being hindered is the fact that the policies used today were written centuries ago. This is not to say that the founding fathers of this country did not write these policies in great wisdom, but it is to say that life is completely different now than it was then. Society has transformed drastically just in the last hundred years, yet the major polices that control our social structure were written long ago. How can anyone claim that policies written and interpreted in the 1700's are still valid in the twenty-first century?

Take computer technology for example. Imagine if every part of the computer had advanced as it has except for the processor. Computers would be capable of doing many wonderful things, but they would be incredibly slow and virtually useless. The computer would eventually become overloaded and the processor would burn out. Society's current policies are the processor within the sociological computer and, without an upgrade in processing, our social advancement will continue to be impeded and eventual fall apart.

To upgrade our social system, we need to be very critical and carefully analyze the issues. Only through this critical and thorough non-biased evaluation, can the problems be identified properly. Once we have identified the problems, we can begin to fix them. We have no hesitation taking objects that have problems and making them more efficient, but for some reason, we are very hesitant to take a system or a policy with problems and making it better. This, however, is where the most essential growth is needed. Our social efficiency is the catapult for growth that will lead us to far greater technological advances, unlimited sources of energy, financial and social freedom, and above all, true happiness.

If we continue to allow political machination to rule our system, nothing will ever change. A study was done out of Emory University that was to determine the effect politics has on a person's ability to think logically. What researchers found was, when people are faced with absolutely proven facts that contradict their political stance, they shut their minds off and ignore the facts.[25] We need to really think about the significant of this. For example, if the facts and statistics show that a policy in place has had no positive influence on society, people will ignore those facts if their political party supports that policy, and vice versa. When political affiliation can so badly cloud someone's ability to think logically and reason properly, there is a severe problem.

Now as we have established earlier, nearly everything is fueled by greed and envy under our current system. This is displayed on a regular basis by the policies imposed by our politicians and supported by the rich. We also know that policies are neglected or ignored if they are not in the best interest of the richest most powerful people, who control our minds through such politics. Let's look at the impact this has on us. Suppose a man invented a free energy source, a source of energy that could be pulled from Earth's natural pulsating electrical currents. Could you imagine the impact this would have on the all-powerful energy industry? There would be no need for OPEC, and the thousands of oil refineries, and the thousands of drilled oil wells. There would be no need for dams, for coal, and for many other massive pollutants. The results would be great for most of humanity, but terrible for the rich and powerful, who own and control these infrastructures. Since these rich and politically powerful people rule these industries, do you really think this technology would ever be released?

In the late 1800's, Dr. Nikola Tesla discovered a pulsing electrical current that naturally occurs in Earth's atmosphere.[26] He was determined to build a tower to harness this energy and provide free energy to the public, but the government halted his attempt. Instead, his technology was later investigated by Dr. Bernard Eastlund, who passed it on to the U.S. government, where it is currently being used to conduct various military related tests using the HAARP (High Frequency Active Auroral Research Program) in Alaska.[27] In an efficient society, this technology would have been harnessed for the benefit of all, and not reserved for government use only.

This is one example, but it would be extremely naïve to think it stops there. Let's discuss the medical field. Prescription drugs are a trillion dollar industry worldwide. Isn't it interesting that a hundred years ago, during our technological infancy, we were able to develop vaccines for small pox, polio and other major diseases, but today we are not able to find a cure for any major diseases? Our scientists have no problem finding treatments that require long-term payments, and billions of dollars worth of health-care products, but they just cannot seem to find a cure.

Consider how many people have cancer alone. If cancer was cured tomorrow, imagine the financial impact that would have on the world. Hundreds of billions of dollars spent on treatments and drugs would no longer be necessary. The thousands of scientist worldwide who are "searching" for a cure would have to find something else to research. Perhaps these scientists are only looking for ways to control the cancer, not cure it, because they know that if they cure cancer they are out of a job and hundreds of billions of dollars are lost. It is hard to imagine the capabilities scientists have developed, but are not allowed to distribute publicly, because of the greed and power of the people controlling these technologies. The bottom line on this is always money. Once this greed is eliminated and efficiency is achieved through a new social system, these technologies will be released and we will see unbelievable growth in all fields, in our families, and within ourselves.

Most politicians are concerned with two things, filling their pockets and retaining their power. These are the reasons people pursued political power from the beginning, and they are still the same reasons today.[28] So when politicians are faced with a crisis or a public outrage, they quickly enact policies that are not well thought out, just so they can say they are doing something about the crisis. They do not necessarily want to solve the problem; they want to say, "Look, we are trying." This is how our government officials are hindering our social efficiency. Today we are facing more and more problems from every possible source, and these quick fixes are now causing more problems than they are correcting.

Think of our current governance as the wall of a dam being flooded with hoards of new issues. As the wall ages and become inundated by issues, they produce cracks representing problems. Instead of analyzing the issues in depth and building a new and improved wall to accommodate these problems, government officials have continued to patch the cracks with quick, but brittle fixes. If the same wall continues to be used, the cracks that are patched will continue to spring new leaks, and continue to get bigger until the wall finally collapses completely.

An efficient society will not be flooded by new issues, but will embrace new issues and use them as opportunities to grow and become more efficient. These new issues will not be overwhelming, because our new level of social efficiency will be ready to accommodate them.

Once we have achieved this social efficiency, we will begin to excel at a tremendous pace. We will excel so rapidly because all people will contribute in one form or another to the whole of society, rather than trying to manipulate and outdo each other. Currently, our system produces the notion that if you do not work you will be poor, living on the street, and struggling to provide for yourself and your family. The more liberal policies say, "If you are struggling, we will support you while you struggle." The moderate policies say, "We will support you as long as you try to find work." All of these policies are either quick-fix policies to make it look like the government cares, or "figure it out for yourself" policies from politicians who care nothing about society, only themselves.

When we care nothing about other people, we fail to realize the ubiquitous laws of cause and effect and the reaction they have. As explained earlier, these are the universal laws that affect us in every way, physically, psychologically, financially, and socially. Everything we do, or don't do, has an equal and opposite reaction somewhere or on someone else. The truth is that *we are personally responsible for everything that is happening. We create our own happiness, but more importantly,* **we create the very problems we complain about.**

When we can break from our individual, self-centered ways, we begin to realize that by helping the whole, we are helping ourselves. We realize that for every person that is not contributing, our system is losing, and therefore we too are losing. We are losing money paying for welfare, we are losing productivity, we are losing time with our families, and we are losing ourselves.

Is not the goal of producing more efficient technology to make life easier by getting more things done faster? Our technology is becoming rapidly more successful at this objective, but our social system is not. As defined, the purpose of efficiency is to get more done, while saving time and effort. But what is the purpose of saving time and effort through efficiency if our social system is not going to adjust in a manner to harness it?

We have lost sight of this objective and instead filled the time we have saved with more effort and more work, because we have been taught that we must work harder and longer hours to be considered an asset to the company. In the back of our minds, we have the dreaded science fiction notion of a robot taking our jobs and leaving us jobless. We think we need to work twice as hard and twice as long to prove that we are important. When we know a machine can be built to do the job of 100 men at five times the pace, we wonder when the day will come that our employers don't need us.

However, this is only a fear under our current system. This is a fear brought about by owners who constantly ask for more, while offering less, and a fear that allows people in power (the wealthy) to take advantage of those who are not. When we have achieved social efficiency, we will have no problem with machines doing

work for us, in fact, we will strive to create more machines that can do more of the work for us, because we
will still get paid, and we will all be contributing in one
way or another to the efficiency of society.

Chapter 5
How To Change

SOLUTION 1: JOB SHARING

Full Employment

To achieve this new system, we must understand that as society becomes more efficient there is less need for each person to work. Going back to our computer processing example, the more advanced processors become, the more information they can process and the less energy it takes. Soon we are going to have to accept that society is capable of processing (accomplishing) much more with much less effort. So how do we balance this? How do we accommodate this leftover time, when our efficiency allows us to finish so much more with less effort and in a shorter amount of time? How is it possible to develop a system far more efficient than we have now and still accommodate the millions of people who do not have jobs under our current inefficient system?

The beauty of social efficiency is that we are able to solve many problems with one simple adjustment: we share jobs and we work less, by rotating workers within the same jobs. Rather than having one CEO, we have three CEO's all paid the same, but they alternate time on the job and time on vacation. Under our current system, in 2008, the average CEO's pay decreased by 15 percent to an absurd $9.5 million, according to the NY times.[29] In an efficient society, we would have a nation-wide salary cap, including CEOs at say, $250,000 a year. Limiting a CEOs salary to $250,000 a year now provides thirty-eight more positions paying the same $250,000 a year. That is, if the thirty-eight jobs were CEO positions. The general work force would have lower salaries, allowing up to one-hundred and ninety jobs making $50,000 a year or more, by simply eliminating the greed among CEOs. The best part is, because society is so efficient, we are all on the work clock for only a fraction of the time. This leaves a tremendous amount of time for us to live life to its fullest. We now have leisure time to read, to take classes, to travel, and most importantly to spend with our families.

It is completely unnecessary that an employee works 60 or even 40 hours a week. I share with you this fact: You are overworked for one purpose, to save the company money. It is far cheaper to make you work extra, than to hire a second person. Businesses know this and that is why they continue to overwork everyone. The truth is, the more you work, even if you are making more money, the company is making even more. The solution comes by splitting jobs, working fewer hours, and implementing salary caps. This provides people with more time for themselves and their families, creates less stress and more jobs thus lowering or eliminating unemployment, and minimizes the wealth gap, which has created the large number of problems that stem from greed and envy.

In his book, "The World is Flat," Thomas Friedman discusses an incident that occurred in India, where they have more highly skilled and educated people than they know what to do with. In this particular situation, there was a job fair where a company needed to fill 9,000 computer-engineering jobs. They had over one million qualified applicants apply. Needless to say, they were able to select the cream of the crop from a large number of highly skilled people, but 991,000 highly qualified engineers were left jobless.[30] Why does it have to be this way? I am not aware of the occupational expectations of these 9,000 new hires, but I assume they included at least the standard American 40-hour week. It's likely that it turned out to be more in the range of 60-80 hours per week, and for a tenth of the pay of an American engineer. Though we do not have this degree of a problem in the U.S., we still have a lot of highly skilled and educated people not utilizing their abilities.

In an Efficient Society, this will not occur. If a company like Intel employs five million engineers nationwide, this number can easily be doubled or tripled by splitting the labor and sharing jobs. This coincides directly with the question, what will we do with all of the extra money? We will create jobs. The easiest way to fathom this is to picture every single occupation on a university-like schedule, broken into three trimesters. Depending on the efficiency of the company on its own, it could employ up to three people for every job. Each person would work on site for a trimester, off site for a trimester (possible doing research or just working on a project as a hobby), then have the third trimester off completely. This would leave each of them with more time for their families, more time for innovation, and provide the company with a wider range of skills and brain power to consult. After all, two heads are better than one.

Wider Skill Base and Brain-Power

Who hasn't heard the phrase, two heads are better than one? I wanted to put this idea to the test, so I took a close relative of mine, gave him an IQ test, and recorded his score. I also gave his wife an IQ test and recorded her score. Then I gave a completely different IQ test to both of them at the same time. I asked them to collaborate and answer only after they had both agreed on the answer. The results were drastically better on the collaborated effort. In this one case, the score was 65 points better than the lesser of the individual IQ scores and 50 points better than the higher of the two IQs. What was even more impressive was the actual collaborated score. With a combine IQ of 175, these two heads together would be considered a genius. This collaborated effort can be applied to any job scenario and shows how job sharing and building off the intelligence of two or three minds produces a much more powerful and efficient result.

The Lump of Labor Theory

Job sharing is by no means a new idea. Economist Dr. David F. Schloss coined "The Lump of Labor Theory" that suggests that the number of possible jobs is fixed, and therefore we will eventually have to share jobs, since we will not be able to employ everyone otherwise.[31] I am not suggesting we have reached our labor threshold. In fact, I do not believe in this theory at all, because it does not take into account how innovative the human mind can be, which also contributes to job creation.

When technology increases, it sparks new ideas, and these new ideas create new job opportunities, new realms of study, and new expertise. As life and nature changes, the same thing occurs. For example, a hundred years ago there were no computer engineers, no aeronautical engineers, no rocket scientists, and certainly no one pursuing the multiple avenues of green energy, which is set to produce a completely new direction of engineering. We will always be creating new branches of occupation, and therefore we will always be adding more jobs.

Instead, what I am saying is we are wasting our brain-power; we are wasting our lives, and our human potential on jobs that can be performed by machines. When we are not providing our educated citizens with jobs within their areas of expertise that they are passionate about, we are wasting their potential and our efficiency is lost. There are millions of brilliant people with advanced educations who are doing sales, working retail, or pushing envelopes. This is like using super glue to stick two pieces of paper together; it is a waste of a stronger resource, when you could use a different resource like tape. I am not suggesting that job sharing will solve all of our economic problems; rather, I am explaining that jobs should be shared so that we can become a more efficient society. This would harness all of our intellectual resources, provide workers more time for themselves and their families, and give our citizens a better quality of life.

The Benefit of Time for Families

One of the biggest social issues to arise in the last several decades concerns the structure and responsibility of the family. Children are not being raised well because parents are spread so thin. With so much emphasis put on working more to make more money, many adults do not have the time to focus on their relationship with their child and spouse. Psychologist and sociologists have many reasons why children have become menacing and why the divorce rate has jumped so high in the past few decades. However, no matter what data they throw at us, it most often comes back to one underlying factor; people don't have time for each other anymore.[32] The more time married people spend away from each other, the more they grow apart, and eventually they may separate completely. Not only is the bond between husband and wife weakened through so much work, but children suffer as well.

Children growing up today lack guidance from home and the effects of this are terrible. When parents are not there to mentor their kids and be role models for them, the kids turn to outlets such as television, peers, and even worse, drugs. We wonder why kids are so disrespectful, just look at their role models. On television we have an NBA player making millions of dollars a year who is recorded telling sports reporters to "F-off." Musical artists are admired for their talents, yet some use this fame to promote sex, drugs, gang activity and even killing people.[33]

In the old days, mom would stay at home to care for the kids. In the present era this is very rare. The Efficiency Theory offers something far better. With job sharing, both parents will have time for their children, either together or at alternating times. The Efficiency Theory shows that, as society reaches higher levels of efficiency, parents will be able to alternate being at home with the kids, or even plan time together for long family vacations. It is time we reap the benefits of thousands of years of technological advancement. Considering all of the technological advances to date, there is no reason we are still set up in the same manner as the 1800's. It is time we embrace our advances and enjoy the benefits of our achievements. Looking again to the laws of cause and effect, as we alternate working times, we will have much more time for our families. Family bonds will grow stronger than ever before. As a result, divorce rates will drop, children will be raised better, and our time together will be much more valuable. The Fair Compensation Act will also ensure that we have the money to enjoy our time off, and not be burdened by constant financial worries.

One question I have been asked is; how will advances come so quickly when people are working less? Let me remind you that many of the greatest technological and medical advances have come not from a single man diligently working for a solution, but from many men, each picking up where others have left off. It is also important to understand that when people love their work, they will continue to work in their spare time because, like a hobby, it is their passion. Just ask any coach of a high school or little league sports team. There is often little if any pay for these people, yet they volunteer their time because they enjoy it or they take pleasure in providing this service for kids. When we are doing the things we love to do, we never stop doing them, regardless of the compensation.

On Innovation

As I was discussing the Efficiency Theory with a fellow educator in the Social Sciences, he brought up an extraordinary point. We were discussing why so many major life-changing inventions that are still in use today were invented around the same time period. The light bulb, electricity, the telephone, and the internal combustion engine for cars are just a few of the innovative technologies from that era that had a profound impact on society. What was so special about that time period? Why is it that today most inventions are relatively less significant, and the ones that are significant seem to be

programs invented by college students or recent graduates who had been working on ideas throughout their
college careers? During that time period, the industrial
revolution was at full force, which meant, for the first
time in history, machines were making life easier, more
efficient, and people had more time to THINK.

When a person's life revolves around farming and
every waking moment is spent working and trying to
survive, there is not much time to invent something.
The industrial revolution essentially provided people
with the tools that made life more efficient. As a result
of this efficiency, the people had more time to think
and invent.

When our minds are preoccupied with mundane
work, we fail to use the creative parts of our brains. Take
Isaac Newton for example, was he in a laboratory when
he discovered the notion of gravity? No. Did ancient
Egyptians invent the wheel so they could patent it and
make millions of dollars? No. These people saw a cause
and contributed to the society for the purpose of social
efficiency.

It is also important to point out that many discov-
eries are made during leisure time, because the brain
is not overwhelmed with the stress of deadlines and
quotas. Studies have shown that the brain functions at
far more optimal levels when it is rested. Scientists have
looked at the study habits of students and found that
those students who studied more while resting less
actually did worse on exams than those who stopped
studying at a reasonable time and got enough rest. The
study showed that the first group suffered from men-

tal burnout.[34] "Burnout" has become a far more prevalent word in today's society, because people are overworked. Under social efficiency, burnout will cease to exist and we will accomplish more while working less.

Today, many of society's smartest and most educated people are working long, hard days for a company that is pushing them to work more, and giving them less time to think. Sure, we have more tools now that make life easier and more efficient than in the industrial revolution era, but peoples' lives are still filled with work. There are still thousands of people inventing things every day. However, most of the inventions today are inspired by the potential wealth they may bring, and many of these inventions are based on copycat ideas and fads.

To see an example of this, all you have to do is watch the many info-mercial that are on television every Sunday morning. These commercials are filled with different home-exercise machines that guarantee great abs, or the best full-body work out, or with numerous stain removing products that are guaranteed to clean any stain. You see this because people don't have time to really think up an original thought; instead, they copy ideas and add a twist. The motive is not to make a better product, but to sell something that might catch on and make them a lot of money. People today care more about personal wealth than about the health, safety, or prosperity of humanity. We need to channel this inventive energy, and direct it toward more innovative, problem solving, and humanity serving inventions.

We are currently experiencing a technological revolution that will keep our heads spinning for years. As machines begin to do more for us, in less time and with less effort, this will make more time available for us to *think* of new things and new inventions. We need the extra time to think so we can capitalize on this new era. Job sharing will provide society with the means and the time to allow this to occur.

Solution 2: Changing Perception

Purpose Driven Work

To take the large leaps necessary toward achieving our ultimate efficiency, we need to focus on *purpose* in our work, rather than pay. There are actually quite a few individuals willing to give up some of their financial desires to perform an occupation that they are either very passionate about, or believe important enough to overlook inferior compensation. Take a teacher for example: In terms of relative educational attainment and duties, teaching is a very low-paying profession. According to research at payscale.com, in 2008, a teacher with a bachelor's degree, in the United States, earned a salary between $36,000 and $42,000 a year. In comparison, accountants or computer science graduates with a bachelor's earned between $46,500 and $77,500 and $56,400 and $97,400 a year respectively.[35] These professionals pay the same tuition and attain the same number of credits, but one is certainly not compensated as well as the other.

However, there are millions of teachers who will continue to teach because they believe in the importance of their job to society. Now, let's compare a doctor and a teacher with a Ph.D. (comparable education levels). Medicine is an extremely noble profession as well, but is it more noble than teaching? A doctor's job is to preserve life, while a teacher's job is to guide and help others to create their lives. Imagine where you would be without the teachers who taught you what you know. We would not have doctors without teachers to pass on the knowledge and expertise that teach the doctor how to be a doctor. Without teachers, a person's ability to understand and function through the daily activities of life would be limited.

We link a certain value to a certain job. For example, many people would argue that if doctors and other high-paying jobs did not pay so well, then nobody would put out the effort in education and advanced training to become one. Why then does teaching defy this argument? Why don't we hear people saying, "If teachers didn't get paid enough, no one would be a teacher?" The answer is, because *it is simply not true*, and it would not be true for doctors either. The main reason this is true, is because we have placed an expected value on these professions. If we were born into a society where the salaries for these careers were reversed, then our expected pay to be a doctor would be much lower and our expected pay to be a teacher would be much higher; it is simply a matter of a perceived expectation.

There are, in fact, many people who have gone through school to be teachers and after their first year of teaching, decided it was not for them. They left teaching either because the pay was bad, they could not handle the stress of trying to manage insubordinate kids, they felt threatened by gang violence, or because they did not find it fulfilling. Those who stick around to teach do so because they believe they can make a difference. They believe their life's purpose is to contribute to the future of society by helping children develop into successful adults. These people will continue to teach regardless of the pay. Those who left the profession would have likely been poor teachers anyway, because their interest was in something else, they could not handle the job, or they did not truly have the passion to begin with.

Doctors do not have the turn-over rates that teachers have primarily because of the amount of specialized education they had to attain, the number of hours they put in for residency, the amount of money they make, and the fact that many are passionate about saving lives. Although, even if doctors were not passionate about saving lives, they would have a tough time leaving their profession, because it would be difficult to justify unless they moved into a field of research with similar pay. A teacher can simply leave their $36,000 to $42,000 a year job and make more money in a sales position, that doesn't even require a degree. A doctor on the other hand would have a difficult time finding a job to replace their salary.

This actually creates a serious problem, because any time you have people doing something only for the money, or because they feel they have to, they will not be doing it to the best of their ability. We could easily have a whole slew of doctors who don't really care about you or I, or even about helping the sick. Such doctors may care only about their pockets and paychecks. If doctors were paid half of what they currently make, would there still be doctors? You bet! The good ones would stay. Those that would leave the profession are those who cared only about the pay anyway, and not about helping people. Likewise, would more people strive to become teachers if the pay was better? Absolutely, but you would likely have a ton of people who would move into the profession for the money, and not to make a difference.

The fact is, our external reward system, has trained us to care about the pay we receive and not the product we produce. When it is the external reward that gives us the motive to work, the results of our work never reach their full potential and our efficiency is decreased. If you believe that this is the way it has to be to get people to work, consider the research.

Researcher Edward Deci found in one study that paying students to perform actually decreased their motivation. In the study, students were divided into two groups. They were give several interesting puzzles and asked to solve them. One group would be paid a dollar for each puzzle they completed, while the other group would be paid nothing. The results showed that the students who were paid to perform did just enough work to solve the puzzles and stopped, while the other group continued to play with the puzzles even after they were finished.[36] This demonstrates the psychological consequence of externalizing the value of an effort. When that value is internalized, the excitement continues, the intrigue is expanded, and the effort performed is greater and lasts longer.

Let's take a few other examples from the acting profession and from sports. There are many stories about famous actors who lived in poverty, even out of their cars, at some point in their lives before they made it big. The vast majority of actors are not paid large sums of money for their work, but they continue to act, often for little or no compensation. Many of these actors, working in plays or local shows, have a second job to pay the bills while they act. They continue to act because they love to do it. If actors and actresses in Hollywood were paid a decent salary regardless of their popularity, ranging from $50,000—$150,000 a year, instead of the grossly overpaid millions some get, would they quit acting? Absolutely not!

They are paid to do something they love to do and are extremely passionate about. It is likely that most of them acted for fun in high school plays or in college. At that point, they did it for nothing more than the love of it. The amount of money paid to top Hollywood actors is absurd. Over time, the media has created a grotesque perception of wealth in Hollywood, as actors and actresses have flaunted it all over the world. This has created an expectation of wealth that has adulterated the profession altogether. However, rest assured that the best actors, those who truly love doing it, would continue to do it regardless of the compensation.

Professional athletes are no different. I would be amazed if any professional athlete said they did not love playing their sport. They live the ultimate dream, to do something you love to do and be well compensated for it. Do you think for a moment, if every athlete in professional sports were paid $100,000 dollars or even $50,000 dollars a year instead of getting multimillion dollar contracts, that they would quit the game? Absolutely not! There are so many other factors motivating these people to play. Many love their sports; others love the fame. Let's not forget that all throughout their childhoods, these same athletes were paid nothing to play these sports. In many high schools and little league sports, participants are required to pay to play, and many adults who love sports pay organizations that run sports clubs because they love to play.

If we have so many people who love sports enough to pay to play, then why do other athletes not only get paid, but paid absurd amounts of money? The answer is; because we accept it and allow it. Money has only become an issue in professional sports and acting because it is allowed and flaunted, which has resulted in an expected level of pay. It has become a status symbol to show that player X is better than player Y because they are paid more. It has, in fact, adulterated the purity of the sports and the arts and dampened the passion and purpose these people hold. Once we cap salaries, compensating them no differently than other professions, the truly passionate athletes will reign and the purity of the sports will return.

Determining Value

One question remains with this theory: Since our society was built on centuries of training people to be greedy, won't people always want more money? In general, people simply desire happiness. People want to do something that they love to do, something they enjoy and something that makes them feel good about themselves. Even in America's most difficult economic times, when people are asked what would make their lives better 67% ranked "more free-time" most important, according to Pew Research Center of Social and Demographic Trends.[37] Most people truly understand that money cannot buy happiness. Rather, they seek more because of the envy that television, the internet, and ingrained social conditioning has coaxed us into believing. It is our most primitive instincts involving competitiveness that advertisers prey on. They provoke public greed to support their personal greed, and this cloud of greed blocks our minds from seeing what truly makes us happy.

The good news is that we have actually learned to control these instincts in many respects. The proof is in our history. Long ago, status was proven through physical fighting, between individuals and through battles between groups. Through time and increasing civility, we now strive to attain status through other means. Today, that means is money. This is why people flaunt their wealth. When we see people today displaying flashy clothing, fancy cars, and big houses, it is really no different than men flaunting their muscles or swords in the past. This is where they find power and prestige.

There is an unfortunate consequence to this situation. When people are preoccupied with flaunting their material wealth, they are drawn away from their passions into seeking status through disposable means. Once we transform the idea of status away from the trained belief that money is the way to prove we are of value, and replace this notion with a belief that value is to be found in purpose and self-fulfillment, we will begin to see a new era of achievement.

Perception of ownership

One of the first major changes that needs to occur is in how people perceive the idea of value and worth. Ownership has taken on a controlling function in society, because it contributes to our greed and envy in the most powerful way, by allowing people to flaunt their wealth. People use what they own to publicly display their value. This is used to justify the separation of people by dividing them on a social and personal level.[38] When we divide people and classify them based on what they own, we add to the pervasive problems associated with greed and envy. Thus, the pendulum of cause and effect gains momentum.

Ownership has become symbolic of greed and it compels people to express dominance over others. Those people who own the most are placed on a pedestal, by themselves and often times by others, because people equate a person's value to what they own. In fact, the question, "What is your worth?" almost always refers to financial value. This implies that a person who owns more is of greater value to society, and is therefore better than, someone who owns less.

What many people fail to perceive is that ownership is not absolute. The only thing we have absolute ownership of is our thoughts, and now that we understand how teaching, advertising, and social conditioning influence our thoughts, even that can be considered questionable. Picture two men sitting next to each other in a coffee shop, one is dressed in old, torn jeans and a plain white t-shirt, while the other is dressed in an Armani suit with gold chains and a personalize gold-lined coffee mug. When asked which of these men are worth more, many people would probably say the well-dressed man. However, what they may not realize is that this man has unethically made his way to wealth by cheating people out of their passions, while the first man has donated his wealth in service to humanity. We judge things based on a face-value perceptions, which are provided by beliefs ingrained by commercials and media. Here is what media doesn't show us: the first man is a paramedic who lives very modestly as he spends most of his hard-earned money providing food and shelter for the local orphans. When he is not working for as a paramedic, he spends his time teaching the orphan children for free. The second man has made millions of dollars by selling what he claims are "five star personalized business plans" to people, but he really just puts a few provided facts into a template and prints out the plan. And, only a very small percentage of the business plans get a second look from investors. Our conditioned impression based on wealth in ownership would never reveal the true value of the first man. The two will continue their lives and most people will always assume the man who owns the flashy items is more valuable, because of his appearance.

The irony is that ownership is nothing more than an illusion. No one truly owns anything. People who want to claim ownership of something fail to realize that every item that someone owns today will one day be "owned" by someone else. Once you have sold an item, it is no longer personal property. The time that item was in your possession was technically the equivalent of renting or leasing it. Some people have realized this and it has spawned the idea of leasing. In fact, more people in the world rent homes, cars and other necessary items than own them, because the reality is that no one really owns anything.

Take a house, for example; millions of people in the last century have pursued buying a home out of the desire to call a place their own. Now let's look at the reality of purchasing a home. Most of us will never actually own a house in our entire lives. Most people will have a mortgage until the day they die and, when that happens, their next of kin will either sell the property to try to make some money, or the bank will take the property back. The reality is that, after decades of making payments, you never really owned your home; it was more like an investment lease.

Now let's say, for the sake of argument, that you are one of the rare people who actually did pay off your home before you died. What has this really accomplished other than build up a bundle of equity in something that you want to say is yours? When you die, it will go to someone else, just as everything we want to claim we own will eventually go to someone else as well. Once we realize this, it is easier to accept that "ownership" is simply a word we use to justify commitment. In buying a house, we accept a commitment to pay someone else money (most likely a bank), with the deal that while we live there we can call it our own. The only difference with renting a home is that you are paying a third party, paying a person who will then turn around and pay a bank. But once again, no one really owns anything.

Ownership is concept that we invented to assure security. We feel better when we can call something ours and know that we can have it, use it, and modify it at will. However, it is important to realize that, even under today's system, the concept of ownership varies tremendously depending on the object and length of time it is being owned. I had a friend that saved for quite some time to purchase his dream vehicle, a hummer. When he first bought the vehicle, no one was allowed to drink in it and he would not let anyone drive it. After about nine months, he started to let people drink in it, eat in it, and drive it all the time. This temporary extreme care for what we own occurs quite often when it is new to us. But the mind quickly realizes that the item is not that important, which shows is that ownership is actually a very weak concept. When you look at the big picture, you can easily begin to see that nobody really owns anything. I own my house, but I am paying a mortgage so actually the bank owns my house. I own my car, but I won't want it forever, so I really just paid to use it until I moved on to something else.

When you die, nothing you own will matter anyway, so this concept of ownership is really quite silly. An efficient society will realize these are the facts of life and we embrace them. We will use this realization to our advantage and we will no longer be concerned with the concept of ownership. We will realize that this illusion of ownership has actually impeded our growth as a society by consuming us with the false idea that the wealthy can call so much "their own." These people, however, can only call more items "their own" due to the seemingly unlimited salary potential our current system allows. Within the efficient society, this will cease to exist because The Fair Compensation Act will prevent such superfluous spending. People will realize that they do not need to claim ownership to flaunt their personal value, but will seek value in personal fulfillment and successfully using their passion to contribute to the efficiency of society.

Understanding Social Efficiency

If we are going to take the right steps to becoming a more efficient society, then we need to change. We need to eliminate the natural tendency we have to outdo everyone else and constantly try to prove our worth through material items. We need to focus on how everyone's worth is interrelated and on how our value is measured by our combined output. However, if this self-righteous, greedy tendency is an instinct conditioned by millions of years of evolution, and if it has been at the forefront of our social conditioning to get us to work harder, then how do we change? The same way we eliminated our barbaric instinct in the name of being humane and civil; we make it illegal. We make it policy.

When people first read *The Efficiency Theory,* they may be turned off by the idea of salary caps and by the notion that ownership is really just an illusion. Again, people fear what they do not understand, and they find reason to prevent anything new from arising. So the first criticism is always that this sounds a lot like communism and communism didn't work.

Let me explain how this is different from communism. In communism, the government has control of all of the money. This means, if productivity increases as the people work, the money is taken from them and redistributed as the government pleases, mostly into government officials' pockets. There are no salary caps in communism, because there are no "salaries," *per se.* People are given allowances and food coupons, and discretionary money rarely even exists for the people. When it does, it is very little and is already accounted for in the family bills. In communism the government says, "We get all of the money, and we will take care of the people."[39]

In the market economy, it is the business owners who get all of the money, and they say, "No, we will not take care of the people. We will make you work as we say and pay you what we feel you are worth, but most of the money stays with us." Either way you look at it, some group of people are at the top hoarding the money and distributing it to the workers as they see fit.

In Western society, we have just been taught to believe that it is fairer when businesses determine our worth. In the Efficient Society, there is no one company, CEO, government official, or politician at the top hoarding all of the money. The money is distributed to every working person by salary, within a relatively moderate range, based on educational attainment, degree of difficulty, stress, and productive impact, defined by a national salary scale.

In the Efficiency Theory, nothing is ever taken or given to one entity like the government. Instead, it is the same amount of money, still publicly owned, and it is simply in the hands of many rather than the hands of few. Think of the United States as one giant business instead of businesses within a business. Rather than trying to destroy each other and take business away from each other, we are working together to create one great corporation. We no longer need to try to put each other out of business. We have plenty of foreign businesses to compete with for this. Instead, we work together as efficiently as possible, as one singular efficient system.

This firm has everything the other firm had except this firm is much more efficient because we have people doing jobs that they love to do. They are passionate about their success in these jobs and work hard because, to them, it isn't really work at all, it's "my purpose." The difference now is that people can do the things they love to do, because there is not the stress over having enough money. One single athlete, who currently makes a $4 million salary, will now make $100,000 a year, and the remaining $3.9 million will provide 39 passionate researchers $100,000 a year salaries, or 52 passionate teachers $75,000 a year salaries, or 78 city service jobs $50,000 a year salaries.

If this sounds crazy, ask yourself: Who in their right mind wouldn't play basketball, if it is their life's passion, for $100,000 or even $50,000 a year? And who couldn't live comfortably on a minimum salary of $50,000 a year. Remember, the only reason it is hard to imagine a basketball player playing for $100,000 a year is because of the perception we have been taught to hold currently. If this is how it was for everyone, do you think professional sports would just disappear? Not a chance. Athletes would still love to play, and they would be playing for the passion of the sport.

Solution 3: The Fair Compensation Act

A National Salary Scale

We must implement a nation-wide salary scale that covers all occupations. Years ago, the big talk in baseball was a system called salary caps. What a grossly ridiculous thing to consider $5,000,000 a salary cap, but the thinking is right. To assure all people are able to live comfortably, nation-wide salaries could range between $50,000 and $250,000 per year, with the national salary cap set at $250,000 per year (These numbers are used to simplify the example; more appropriate numbers could be determined by economic specialists).

Now imagine a society where no single family is making less than $50,000 a year with one parent working and none less than $100,000 a year with both working. Poverty would no longer exist and theft would be unnecessary. This would also minimize the absurd income gaps between the rich, the poor, and the middle class, shrinking the gross imbalance in material ownership, and therefore decreasing the fire behind greed, namely *envy*. This distribution of wealth would increase the standard of living enormously, as even the lowest paying tier would still provide a good income.

With this change, two major questions immediately come to mind: 1) Will there be enough money? and 2) If there is too much money, what happens to the money left over? To answer the first question, yes. There will be more than enough money. According to Forbes

Magazine, in 2009, there were 403 billionaires in the U.S.,[40] while Businessweek, estimated 7.8 million millionaires for the same year. Let us not forget that these people are not *just barely* making a million or a billion dollars, but many of them are worth hundreds of millions and tens of billions of dollars. Then there are the are another 12.7 million people making over $500,000 a year plus more nearly 50% of households reported making between $50,000 and $250,000 a year, according to the 2008 U.S. Census.[41]

If you are still not convinced, this does not include the trillions of dollars wasted by the government and businesses that we never hear about because it is laundered, hidden, used as business expenses, and never claimed. When we cap salaries to a reasonable amount and start distributing salaries more evenly and efficiently, the real concern will be what to do with the money left over. So, the more important question is, what do we do with the extra money?

Again, it is important to understand the big picture. Some basic fundamentals of the current system will still be in place. Professions will still vary in pay, as will different levels of each profession. A management position for example, will be compensated better than an entry-level position. A trash collector, will not have the same salary as an engineer, and a teacher will not make as much as a brain surgeon. The major difference is in the ridiculous pay gaps between professions and position levels. We will all make a good livable salary; we just won't have the enormous gaps in pay.

By narrowing this gap, we will begin to balance the money distribution and will actually create a major surplus of money. This is because, instead of "the business" doing well and major surpluses of money being hoarded into individual accounts through bonuses for the few at the top, the surpluses will be used to provide upgraded services, building projects, more education, and salaries for new jobs, as more people enter our efficient work force. Over time through upgraded efficiency, this will result in an increase in the nation-wide salary scale.

Competition and Growth

Intellectuals have argued for years that, without competition, there is no drive for growth. At the core of the market economy, we have companies battling to make better products so that the consumer will come to them for their purchases. They argue that one of the major factors for the failure of communism is that, without the competition to strive for riches no one will want push themselves to grow. As I mentioned before, this may hold true in a society where people do not like their jobs and work for the sole purpose to attain a paycheck, but in the Efficient Society, people will be working in the occupations they love, where they are passionate. However, competition will always remain a good thing to prod further efforts. So we will maintain that competitiveness to help us achieve the most efficient society our planet has even known.

It is important to understand that competitiveness is a learned behavior. We promote competitiveness at a young age with sports, grades, in music, spelling bees, classroom contests and other competitions, all in the name of being the best and being recognized. For most of our childhood, money is not even a factor, and we are still competitive and successfully enjoy competing. This will not suddenly fade, as we become adults, just because we have implemented a nation-wide salary scale. Quite the contrary, people will still find competition in whatever it is they do and, when it is something they are truly passionate about, they will desire recognition for their efforts. Again, money is not the reason.

Effective Competition

One major benefit of the free market is the competition it induces. In ancient times, competitions were a matter of life or death. The Mayans had the game of death, the Romans had the gladiators, and the ancient Asian societies had the Kumate (a martial arts fight to the death). As we grew more civilized, by today's standards, we realized that we could not continue these barbaric acts because they were not good for society. However, we do still do have competitions like this today. We have simply structured them with rules and practices such as, padded cages, protective devices, and doctors to keep people alive if they become injured. We call these competitions "sports." Sports are the way our current society contains our barbaric na-

ture, while still providing entertainment and an opportunity for people to push themselves to their limits.

In terms of economic and scientific advancement,
we can draw a parallel from these ancient barbaric
sports. Today, we are still in the primitive stages of economic advancement. The uncivilized way of gaining
wealth is through taking from each other. We fight over
wealth and we compete for dominance over other people through wealth and status. An Efficient Society will
harness this motive for economic competition in the
way sports harness the drive for physical competition,
while maintaining a civilized "fair market" economy.

In an Efficient Society, there will be scientific super
bowls in addition to sports super bowls. Rather than
competing to see who could score the most points in
a game, we would see which community, company,
team, or individual could create the most fuel efficient
vehicle in the world. We could compete to create the
first suborbital airplane that could travel from LA to To-
kyo in an hour or to invent the first solution that can
halt or reverse lymphatic cancer. With goals set, budgets granted, and a timeframe agreed on, each team
would create a product, test and modify it for a given
time, and then enter it into a super bowl of design. Results would be displayed on a daily basis with a grand
championship event to display the final results. This is
the American Idol of the Efficient Society. This is really
no different from watching a group of people singing,
dancing, trying to lose weight, or hitting a ball.

Multiple competitions will be going on simultaneously and editing for television will certainly add some

spice. Imagine this in NFL television format. Week one would involve introducing us to the teams where we are given profiles of scientists including, previous accomplishments, current studies, interests, and his or her role on the project. Week two would show the beginning stages of the experiment, the hypothesis they are trying to prove, the evidence gathering process, and possible problems they may run into. Later weeks would go through the stages of the experimental process and follow the evolution of the challenge, showing which team is in the lead and comparing how each team is doing as they battle against the others. We see this everyday with such relatively trivial activities as modeling, in shows like "America's Next Top Model." The excitement of televised competitions could certainly be applied to something more productive of social value, such as scientific and technological advances. Televising such competitions in an entertaining format would spark interest in kids and lead to even more passion in those fields.

Using contests with Hollywood-style dramatization and media promotion techniques to accelerate progress is not a new concept. In the height of the cold war, the Apollo Project, a race against the Soviet Union to get to the moon, sparked several major breakthroughs in technology.[42] This resulted in breakthroughs in everything from jet propulsion to health monitoring for the astronauts. Technology was forced to advance drastically to achieve the goal of putting a man on the moon.

On October 4, 2004, The X Prize Foundation gave its first award of $10 million to Mojave Aerospace Ventures for developing the first commercial suborbital space craft. Named the Anasari Prize, 26 teams from 7 different countries competed to be the first to develop a craft that could take normal passengers, not astronauts, into space.[43] Unfortunately, after several years of work from some of the most brilliant local and international engineering minds and over $100 million invested in this contest, the public attention given was far less than the contest deserved. Today, The X Prize Foundation continues to create contests and offer prizes for challenges ranging from the sequencing of the human genome to the development of alternative energy sources, but these contests are not sufficiently dramatized to build interest in a broader public. They target only the scientists who are already interested the field and do not effectively build public interest.

If we are to effectively implement positive change in the public, these amazing advances need to be sensationalized. By using Hollywood-style media expertise and a sports-like presentation, such challenges and accomplishments would provide motivation, unity, pride, and even ownership to the public. Just ask any avid sports fan who their favorite sports team or their favorite player is. The internal desire to look up to a hero, to associate with famous people, and to emulate someone we see on television needs to be used to motivate scientific, social, and academic progress and efficiency.

Impassioned Occupations

What about the jobs that no one wants to do? Are there really people who would be passionate about picking up trash, or cleaning septic tanks? In the beginning, it will be necessary to find people willing to do jobs that they may not necessarily be passionate about. Then again, there are always going to be people who just lack passion in general. What we find with such people is that where there is a lack of *passion*, it is easily replaced with *purpose*. If I know I need to work, and I can make a decent living working any job, then I can find purpose in doing the job. Yes, the purpose has been reduced to "receiving a paycheck" and thus lacks passion, but this is inevitable for some people. However, this will be minimized incredibly by the implementation of Efficiency Education, which you will read about in the next chapter. Nevertheless, it will still occur in some cases. Concerning these people, I remind you that hundreds of millions of people today are already in this situation, working jobs without purpose other than to receive a paycheck. With or without purpose, the difference is that, when they are receiving a comfortable paycheck in the efficient system, the job will not seem nearly as bad.

And then we ask the question, how is it fair that someone without a college degree can make nearly the same amount as someone who does have a degree? First of all, fairness is a relative to how it is perceived. Is it fair that what I am passionate about is paid less than what someone else is passionate about? The truth is, it doesn't really matter. If I am doing what I love to do, and making a comfortable living, then I am happy with my life. Remember that the variations in salary will be very small compared to the lopsided salary gaps in today's system. In our current system, there are some people in commission-based sales, who never graduated from college and make more money than doctors, if they are really good at convincing people to buy things. Is this fair?

I also want to remind you that we all have choices. If you choose to overlook your passions and enter the job force in something you find simple, making $50,000 a year, then that is your choice. If that does not appeal to you, then you will pursue a different route. People need to understand that everything in life is a matter of perception. It is also possible that someone may enjoy doing the work that you feel is repulsive, just knowing that they are providing a necessary service towards the ultimate efficiency of society. For example, should a trash collector be looked down upon? Absolutely not, because we know without them, our garbage would pile up and we would be disgusted. Or, we would just have to take the trash to the waste site ourselves. The bottom line is, we should appreciate this service just as much as the other services provided in our society.

Someone may be thinking, why work towards a college degree if I can come right out of high school and make $50,000 a year picking up the trash. Again, I remind you, that in our most efficient society, we see that most people will have passions they want to pursue. It is inevitable that giving up this passion to seek a paycheck doing work we think is simple, but that does not drive us, will result in unhappiness. This will be explored further when I discuss the Efficiency Theory's system of Education. Until then, know that everything will balance out in the end and all people will be rewarded, acknowledged, and compensated in a relatively fair manner, far more than our current system provides.

Business in an Efficient Society

The nature of a successful business is making or buying something at the lowest cost possible and then selling it for more. To do this efficiently, we need to realize that we are a single national business, providing the best of everything for our citizens. Society benefits as a whole when we make everything at the highest quality possible and at the lowest cost possible. We will continue to sell products at increased prices and, with more people being able to afford them, companies will make more money. This will also allow us to make more money from sales to other nations, while keeping prices low at home. In fact, the most efficient societies will be able to produce the highest quality products at a very low cost, and provide them at a lower cost to people within their community or country, while raising the price for people outside their community. When we are providing the best products because they are the most efficiently made products, produced by people who are passionate about what they do, then *Made in America* will become the desired product brand.

Simple Economics

Our national deficit is in the trillions of dollars because we buy more products from other nations than they buy from us. This is because, in general, wealthy people desire the highest quality products, mostly produced in European countries, while the middle and lower class desire cheap products, mostly made in Asian countries. When our imports are higher than our exports, we are losing money, but when our exports are higher than our imports, we are making money. If we look at our system as a whole, we can see how everyone is connected through multiple facets of society, especially economically. We are one business, the American business. When our surplus is strong, we have more money to distribute, which means raises across the board in the national salary scale. It also results in a more powerful and efficient system to produce higher quality products, at lower cost, while giving society a raise. We will always look to find cheaper ways to produce and provide better products for less because this will directly affect you as an individual, and everyone else, as part of the overall community. If productivity is high, perhaps all professions will receive a 5-percent raise across the board, which continues to be a motivator for all professions. If production is low, we are all affected as well. When we realize that every profession is interconnected in one way or another, and we have all people focused on the same goal, working towards the same objective, the power and efficiency we will harness will be incredible.

What about people who don't pull their weight? Just like the group projects we had in high school, someone always ends up doing more work. So we ask, is it fair that we all get the same grade? First of all, we will not all get the same grade. We have already discussed the new order of compensation, where salaries will be arranged by degree, difficulty, expertise, success, and the job's contribution to our overall efficiency. The difference here is that with the salary cap won't allow one person to make five-hundred times more than another, giving such a massive financial imbalance to provoke greed and envy. To further motivate our already efficient system, the systems within the system can offer bonuses. These bonuses would be given annually and could be anything from public acknowledgement to more time off to a modest dollar amount (as long as they are not pushed over the bonus cap for the year, which would be set at no more than a 20% of a person's salary).

It is also extremely important to realize that much of the skepticism people may have towards the Efficiency Theory is due to a perception that is blurred by trying to figure out how these new ideas will work within our current system. To clearly understand the efficient society, you cannot use examples of problems from our current system, because it is the current system that is creating the problems. Once we embrace efficiency and our system changes, these problems will simply no longer exists. They won't exist because most people will be working in desired professions and they will see that all people are compensated fairly. People will appreciate the jobs others do and the services others provide because we will understand that we are all part of one interconnected system. We will understand that everything we do in our personal worlds affects everyone else in the grander scheme of things.

Other Forms of Motivation

Money has been the primary reward in our system for centuries. However, recognition is a priceless reward as well. The Nobel Peace Prize, the Oscars, the Grammys, Teacher of the Year, and so forth are all examples of professional recognition. The people who receive these awards are often the best at what they do and go above and beyond the call of duty. They excel because they have a deeper purpose in their life's work and they love what they do. People who love what they do generally seek satisfaction from the product rather than from financial reward. More often than not, they would simply like to be recognized for their accomplishment. This is a reward that is above all other rewards, acknowledgment for your greatness at doing those things that you love to do. The Efficient Society will understand this and will have the opportunity to acknowledge more people because more people will be working in professions that they are passionate about and, as a result, there will be more achievements to recognize and award.

Happiness is another great reward. Imagine a world where you were not overwhelmed or obsessed with making more money. Forget about picking a major based on the salary you will receive; you would be able to pick a career based on your passion, what you love to do. While interviewing people to get feedback on my theory, I came across a man who spent his entire life preparing to be a doctor, because his parents and he agreed that a doctor's salary would satisfy his desired lifestyle. After eight years of college and several more years of practical experience through residencies and shadowing, he finally got his job. However, what he never shared was that his real passion was for drawing and designing buildings. As a doctor, he was making $250,000 a year, but it was not what he was passionate about. As an architect, he could easily make a comfortable $50,000 a year, just a fraction of his physician's salary, but he would be doing something he loved to do. Would it be worth it to change? This man designed buildings in his free time, and he would fantasize about a career in architecture, but his parents and he, wanted him to make a larger income than architecture could provide.

This story is all too common. The most unfortunate part of this story is that, if there was not such a large gap in salary, he would have had no problem switching to architecture or would have never pursued the medical field to begin with, and today he would be a phenomenal architect doing what he loves and what he is passionate about.

What is tragic is that, when we are not passionate about what we are doing, we do not work to our highest potential. In the Efficient Society, people will not be held back from their passion. There will not be a struggle between wanting to achieve wealth and wanting to do something they are passionate about. People will be working in the careers they love to do, because there will not be such enormous gaps in the pay potential, and all professions will be fairly compensated.

Effect on Crime

According to FBI statistics,[44] the most prevalent crimes in the United States are various types of theft ranging from a common car theft (that occurs every 26 seconds in the U.S.), to identity theft (19,178 per day), to more violent offenses like robbery (1,134 per day).[8] This doesn't even include the millions of undocumented thefts that occur every day, like the bully who steals someone's milk money, the pick-pockets on the streets, or the hustlers in tourist areas. Keep in mind however, that all of these criminals have something in common: they want money. Only in the rarest cases does a theft occur simply for the thrill of harming an individual. In fact, most often the thief doesn't even know the victim. They don't care if it is you, your cousin, or your worst enemy, they steal not to harm but to help themselves.

With the Efficienct Societyin place, there will be no need to steal. We will all be working for the same business with the same goal at hand. When everyone is doing what they love to do and making a sufficient amount of money to live comfortably at lower stress levels, to have more time for themselves and their loved ones, and to travel, the need for theft will diminish to trace numbers.

When Skill and Passions Do Not Match

While discussing this theory with a colleague, he asked, what if I am passionate about something I have no natural skills at? Passion can often overcome skill. In sports for example, often times someone who is passionate but cannot play well, will still develop into a very good player. What makes these situations special is that the struggles these people face to become good, often lead them to become experts at many different levels. I have seen athletes who are passionate become extraordinary coaches as a result of their struggles to play well. This can happen when someone has dedicated themselves to becoming the best at something they were not given the right gifts to excel in. These people often know the game inside and out and can help those who do have the gift excel even more. In the job force we need both. For the greatest potential to be reached, we need the passionate people who struggle to be great and the naturally gifted to team up. The Efficient Society will convey this collaboration and, when this efficient teamwork is achieved, further growth will be exponential.

Entrepreneurship

Entrepreneurship is easiest to tackle when it is looked at as a whole. The basic objective behind entrepreneurship is to build something that others want to buy, or to provide a service that people want, and make a business out of it. There are two main reasons entrepreneurs seek business ventures. One reason is that they are people motivated by money looking for something they can sell, or a service they can provide, to get rich. Many don't particularly care what it is, because they find their passion in the potential monetary reward. This is often where you find copycat businesses, franchises, and other ventures. More importantly, it explains why 80%-90% of businesses fail within the first five years. Do we really need 200 different coffee shops in the same town or 50 different sandwich shops? These fail because money is the driving force.

Fewer people start a business for the second reason, passion, but these are often more successful entrepreneurs. When people are doing a hobby they love, inventing ways to make life easier, or working on something they are passionate about, they are more likely to discover that there is either a desire or a need for their product or service. These businesses tend to flourish because passion is the driving force behind the venture. These people love what they do whether they are making a lot of money or not. They will continue to work beyond normal business hours because they are passionate about what they are doing.

In the Efficient Society, rather than having hundreds of copycat businesses, entrepreneurs will be releasing new and improved products and services because it will be something they have created out of passion and for the love of what they have created. What is even better, they will not have to worry about failure because their products and services will be released as part of the already established National Corporation and will be opened as a subset of the larger whole.

Entrepreneurship will take on a more stable and efficient approach. When a product or service is invented, market testing will occur to establish the potential success of the business. If tested successfully, the entrepreneur will open business and operate it while being subsidized by the system. They will start at the bottom of the salary scale, until profits have increased enough to increase their salary. Their salary will increase by percentage in correlation with the percentage of business profits, until they have reached the salary cap of $250,000. They may also receive bonuses of up to 20 percent of their base salary. The entrepreneur would continue to be in charge of the business, deciding when to hire and how to make the company more efficient. As the business grows and surpasses levels needed to sustain the start-up entrepreneur, the national salary cap will be in place allowing further profits from the business to go back into the Efficient Economy where it can be invested in further job creation and subsidizing other future entrepreneurs.

The Lesson from the Lemonade Stand

I was taking a neighborhood walk one Saturday morning when I saw three small children selling lemonade on the street corner for 10 cents a cup. I purchased a cup of lemonade and I asked them, "Who makes all of the money from your little business?" One kid said, "We all do." I continued by asking, "But who's stand is it, and who is doing the most work?" At this point, the kids became eager to share their business theory with me. One said, "We all helped by making signs, and getting cups and water. Johnny and Paul squeezed the lemons, and Melissa got the sugar." "I mixed the first jar and when it runs out, whoever is selling will mix the next one." "Two of us sell the lemonade while the other two play catch, and then we trade once the sellers get bored." I asked, "But what if one person sells all of the lemonade when it's their turn; shouldn't they get all of the money?" The children looked at me funny and they said, "Sir, it doesn't matter, it's all of our lemonade stand and we all helped put it together, so we share the money." I insisted on providing them with some greedy market strategies like commission sales and investment.

"Don't you worry about one person selling longer than everyone else and not getting paid for all of their work? That wouldn't be fair, would it?" The child answered, "Nobody works longer than the others, because we trade whenever we get bored." I asked, "What if everybody is bored from selling and nobody wants to do it anymore, or what if one of you decided you want to trade after only a minute or two?" He answered by saying, "Sir, this was all of our idea. It's not like any of us have to do it, we want to do it."

This is precisely what shows that the Efficiency Theory will work. These kids displayed an innocent brilliance that all people hold, before they have become conditioned by the selfish, greedy, manipulative society we live in now. When people are doing what it is that they have *chosen* to do, and not what they feel they *have* to do, they are much more productive and willing to work, and they cooperate at a much more effective and efficient level. These children give us hope for the future.

Solution 4: Efficiency Education

The only way people be will happy in what they do, is if they know what they want to do, are taught how to do it effectively, and are fairly compensated for doing it. Since we have taken care of the issue of compensation through the national salary scale, we must now discover what drives people, and educate them to be successful in their passions. This is where Efficiency Education is imperative to our success and happiness.

One of the greatest struggles in our social evolution is trying to figure out where to go with education. In the past, education was a straight road. Discipline was strict, students were taught right from wrong in terms of social norms, and curricular objectives were based on the student's ability to understand as much information as possible. A teacher's job was to supply facts and teach students where and how these facts are used. (The facts taught were based on books written through a very stringent filter to produce a desired perspective. They were taught science through a religious perspective, and taught morals that mirrored the desired social structure of the church. In the past, the bottom line was that people were told what to believe and they were not to question it.)

Today, society is far more diverse and challenging than it was decades ago. We have conflicting beliefs on everything from religion to what freedom really is. Where a short time ago we were not allowed to question authority, now we have nothing but questions for authority. We have schools where teachers have lost all power, administrators who are slaves to a political bureaucracy, and politicians who are demanding a system that will guarantee achievement for every student, without a clear vision of what it means to be successful. The system of old was straight and narrow and extremely efficient at producing the primary objective of conditioning people, but this system is completely ineffective in today's fast-paced, ever changing society.

The objectives then are not the same as the objectives today. As society has evolved, the objectives have been distorted. Teachers are still expected to teach and augment social norms by demonstrating and teaching morals and character, but that is no longer enough. In fact, there is a large movement sweeping across the public schools in America is called, "Character Counts." This is a program implemented into the schools to promote what they call the seven pillars of good character. The irony is, while teachers are expected to condition students to be of standard moral character, we forget that some of the brightest ideas have come out of defiance. For example, Galileo was ostracized for his idea that the Earth is not the center of the universe. Of course, later the theory was proved to be true, which shows that outside-the-box thinking is not always bad. So I invite people to hold a critical attitude toward my theory for a bit, as I explain how our educational system needs to change.

This analysis is similar to what you have read in previous chapters and here is why, education is a direct reflection of society. All schools are essentially miniature communities that reflect the larger community from which they come. It is an undeniable fact that children are a product of their environment and there are numerous examples of this that teachers see on a daily basis. When you have schools that are performing poorly, all you have to do is look at the community they are coming from. More than likely, the community is poor with uneducated parents. When schools are performing well above average, you can bet that the parents are mostly educated, well-paid professionals. Looking at cause and effect relationships that show how education and society are interlinked, it becomes quite clear that, when we become an efficient society, many of these problems will naturally cease to exist. When money is no longer an issue and parents have the time to educate themselves and assist their children, many of these current problems will subside. However, an efficient system will catapult society into even more rapid advancement; therefore, our educational system must be adjusted to keep up.

To combat this problem, I have come up with what I call "Efficient Education." This is a system of education that strives to fulfill the core educational duty the country has, as well as providing personal discovery and purposeful education for the students. The goal is to provide students with the knowledge and guidance necessary to be efficient contributors to society, to make thoughtful decisions, and to experience freedom in their educational endeavors.

Why Education is Failing

There are two major factors that are causing the majority of problems in education today. These two factors are:

1.   The beliefs that educational authorities hold
2.   The way education is structured

There are a vast number of issues in education today, but most of the problems stem from these two primary causal factors. As I strove to find a singular root cause for the problems, I always came back to these two causes. Therefore, both factors must be addressed equally.

Due to the correlation and determinacy of each of these factors, it is virtually impossible to know which problem causes the other. This evokes the following questions: Do educational leaders have original objective beliefs that ultimately form the structure of the educational system? Or: Are the leaders' beliefs created as products of the system, and are they therefore overwhelming biased toward the structure in which they were involved? Regardless of which question we consider most significant, both concepts are deeply related and have an equal causal impact on the multitude of educational problems in America.

Well-educated people, who have successfully mastered the education system, are invariably the ones who structure the schools. As masters of this system, educational leaders have consciously and subconsciously developed many beliefs about the structure of the system. They do so based on their own success in it. This makes it very important to understand the beliefs held by most educational authorities, since they ultimately prescribe the functions of the system. These are particularly concerned with two main categories of beliefs: 1) the purpose of education, and 2) what constitutes success. By analyzing the perceptions and beliefs of educational leaders, we will ultimately be able to determine the effects these beliefs have on education and provide alternative possibilities to assure success for all students.

Beliefs: Determining Success and Purpose in Education

Since changes to the educational system are prescribed and structured by highly educated people, it is through their perceptions that success is determined. This however poses a serious problem in that not all people share their perceptions of success. Many people tie the idea of success to some form of life purpose. For example, an educational leader may find purpose in improving a school's test scores. Producing this improvement constitutes success for them. However, another person may find purpose in raising healthy livestock and, by doing so, they feel successful. The problem lies in the probability that those who run the schools and structure the system do so through their personal perception of success. They do not take into account other perceptions of success held by people who are not educational professionals. This has transformed education into something that is as much a sales promotion as a medium of conveying knowledge. Teachers and educational leaders today not only have to provide an education, but they must also convince kids to believe in its importance.

Teachers and educational leaders are increasingly faced with students who are more concerned with the *reason* for learning the subject, than the knowledge it is providing. The fact is, it is extremely difficult for educational leaders and teachers to get kids to "buy-in" to something they do not find purpose in. There are far too many perspectives on purpose and success to continue education in its current form. The only chance to truly provide success for every student is to drastically change the system at its core. This includes opening educator's minds to perceptual differences, changing some of the long-held beliefs about education, and restructuring the system altogether.

Problems with the Current Structure

Under the current objectives, education will never attain the achievement it pursues. Politicians and leaders have become extremely keen to determine problems within the educational system, but they fail to step outside the system to evaluate it as a whole. Imagine the educational system as a car with many problems. Without stepping back and looking at the car as a whole, it is impossible to find all of the problems. For example, a tire may be flat and once it is fixed, the car will run okay for a while longer. Then the radiator goes bad, so it is replaced. Finally, the brakes go out and must be repaired as well. This goes on and on until someone steps back, looks at the car as a whole and says, "It is time for a new car." This is the same situation our education system is in.

Currently, leaders are selecting problems such as,low test scores, dropout rates, English language learners, and weak science and math programs, but they are ignoring or failing to see the overall problem. Leaders are feeling extreme pressure to make a difference immediately, so they create policies that are often at the expense of the educative objective, in order to say they are doing something about it. The situation has gotten worse as problems multiply and demands become more extreme. This is causing massive stress on teachers, administrators, and budgets, due to the time and cost of implementing these strategies. Leaders continue to find new problems before the previous problems can be fixed or even re-evaluated. This is a futile game of cat and mouse that will continue to deteriorate education in this country. Rather than looking at the big picture and restructuring the system as a whole, they are providing short-term, quick fixes that often exacerbate the situation or even cause new problems.

Society has changed drastically in half a century and, as technological and scientific breakthroughs occur, it will continue to change at an exponential rate. It is time for educational leaders to step back, look at the system as a whole, and realize that education needs a systematic upgrade. Implementation is no longer the solution to educational problems. The system needs to be restructured altogether. It needs to be renewed in a way that will provide ample opportunity for every student to succeed, but through his or her own perceptual filter of success. This is the ultimate objective of student-centered education, and it is time for us to take the next step.

Efficiency Education Structure

The structure of "Efficiency Education" is broken down into a four-tier system, within a full 14-year compulsory education. Students will start by entering into a basic school at what is currently considered the preschool age, approximately 4 years old. Basic School will last for seven years, where the students will be taught all major curriculums and the basic concepts of life. The following three years of school will be Exploratory School, where students will apply the concepts they have learned and expand on them through functional work inside the schools. This will be an integrating process to bring real life purpose to the academics being learned.

For example, students may have a class in industrial arts where a math teacher and a shop teacher teach together. They could implement assignments and teaching strategies to show how geometry is a function of construction. Science could be integrated with physical education, where students could do laboratory experiments where they would use the scientific principles of physics to develop a practical scientific prescription for how to hit a baseball farther. History could be integrated with English to produce writing samples related to doctrines associated with the Civil War. The possibilities are endless.

Throughout basic and exploratory education, the student would also participate in regular academic, psychological, and sociological tests. These tests would only be used to facilitate and guide students towards their strengths and interests. Students would ultimately have the final decision on the path they chose in life. Schools, however, would go to great lengths to provide students with a mass of valid information on where their strengths and interests lie, at both conscious and subconscious levels.

Once the students have finished Exploratory School education and results have been received from academic, psychological, and sociological testing, they would begin the final two stages of efficient public education. First, students would complete two years of a Pre-Mentorship Program. Part of the day or week (according to each school's policies) would be spent in an academic setting, where theoretical and factual book learning would occur. The other part of the day or week would be spent at two or three different occupational settings, which would be linked to the student's strengths and interests. This could be set up where one occupation is chosen purely by personal interest, another by strengths, and a third by a combination of the two.

The occupational setting could be arranged in a way that would provide on-the-job training, as well as educational facets within the job. For example, a mentorship in nursing would not only provide students with the on-the-job procedures that nurses must follow, but they would also be assigned reports and assignments on scientific lab analysis and pathology studies. Another example would be a computer mentorship where a student would learn on-the-job activities and also turn in reports on mathematical, scientific, and technical writing tasks related to the work. This will assure that students are using and expanding on the concepts that are relevant to them and their work, while drawing a purposeful relationship to the schoolwork assigned.

The last two years of Efficiency Education would allow students two options, an Internship Program or a College Preparatory Program. Option one would be a three-quarter time Internship Program, where students would take their background education, developed knowledge, and practical experience, and team up with a professional in whatever field they have been directed to or chosen. For three quarters of the day, students would actively engage in the job, using the knowledge they have learned, developing professional relationships, and building a repertoire of skills in the field. This could even be an opportunity for students to be paid a modest wage until graduation. This would be even more appealing to the students, as research has shown that "more than two-thirds of all high school students work during their senior year." [45] This may also provide more value to a high school diploma, since graduating high school would come with an employer's endorsement.

Once the high school diploma is earned, students would have the choice of attending college and pursuing an advanced degree or going right into workforce in a job that they are fully qualified for. Keep in mind some internships would require an advanced degree, but this experience provides purpose and motivation to pursue to continue on this track. In this case the student's future would be well established and worked out through guidance counseling or with the company for which the intern had worked. This is crucial in providing each student the best possibility for success. Currently, some schools provide career academies. This is not an internship, but a focus of study within a school. Research has shown that these career academies lower drop-out rates and reduce failure among high-risk students.[46] Efficiency education is taking career academies one-step further.

Within the Internship Program, one quarter of the day (approximately an hour and a half) would be set aside for required school attendance. This time would be spent reviewing and expanding knowledge in all curriculums by means of assigning and reviewing independent studies. Several independent studies would be assigned throughout the course of the two years. They would pertain to the intern's job and creatively provide a synthesis of various elements of curriculum and how they are related to the job. Gene Bottoms, a renowned educational researcher, has published data that shows: "Many students thrive in an environment that allows them to pursue a strong academic core with course work aligned to a career focus" and conversely, when fewer career and technical courses are offered, the number of students earning high school diplomas declines.[47] Bottoms's research also found the following work-based learning experience to be associated with higher student achievement: 1) Observing veteran workers in certain jobs; 2) Learning how to do a job from a work-site mentor; 3) Being evaluated according to clear standards; 4) Receiving encouragement from a work-site mentor at least monthly to develop strong work habits and good customer relations skills; 5) Being shown daily or weekly how to use communication skills at the work site.

The second option would be a purely academic route where students would engage in a rigorous College Preparatory Program. This would include all aspects of curriculum, but still prescribe majors based on the information provided by the strengths and interests analysis. Students from either option could attend college upon graduation; however, the pure academic option is intended to reach out to those students who are scholars at heart. These could be future teachers, professors, or researchers. Success would likely be much higher at these schools, because of the choices involved, the motives to succeed, and the students' perception of success.

Grading

Grading in Efficiency Education would become a thing of the past. In this system, teachers would be trained to teach curriculum, and evaluate students' strengths, weaknesses, and interests, and to guide them in the direction of their greatest potential. This isn't to say students' work would not be assessed. The difference is that the assessment would be focused on personal discovery, strengthening students' weaknesses, and guiding students, rather than on labeling them. A visual example of this approach could involve a math assignment in which a student missed three out of ten problems. Rather than the teacher writing, 70%, 7/10, or a C at the top of the paper, the teacher would write, #3, #5, #10, along with a brief written assessment. The assessment could read: strengths in multiplication and addition, weaknesses in long division and carrying numbers. This turns the student's attention from the negativity associated with being right or wrong to a more positive focus on what is working, what isn't working, and why. This is where a tremendous psychological adjustment can occur.

Ultimately, Efficiency Education is the epitome of student-centered and individual learning. Purpose is arguably the greatest motivator in a person's life. Today, the structure of education is perceived by students as work without purpose. There is no personally recognized purpose in what they do. They experience the "purpose" of schooling as something imposed by educational leaders, that they are forced to do, which contributes to the problem of unmotivated students. They are taught a generic form of success, set by politicians and educational leaders, and prodded in this singular direction. This is no longer working and it needs to be changed. If we can bring purpose to education and if students believe in what they are doing, the face of education will be changed forever.

As the system of education changes, society will follow. The changes that need to occur in efficiency education are the same changes that we need to see reflected in other social functions to produce our Efficient Society. People will feel purpose in their educational experience because they will be learning about things they are passionate about guided by where their subconscious interests and skills have directed them. This will result in unprecedented graduation rates since students will be graduating and pursuing careers in fields the are passionate about, naturally skilled in, and where they are likely to be successful. The focus will also have been taken away from good/bad, right/wrong, and put instead on what works and doesn't work. This effectively trains people not to blame, deceive, and take advantage of others, but instead to coordinate, cooperate, and support each other to achieve success together. The mind set will then be centered on how we can be more efficient as a social whole.

School Calendar

In an efficient school system, the school year will be set up to balance school time with family work schedules to optimize family time together. The traditional school year consists of 180 school days plus 80 days off (not including weekends). This is generally broken down into 3 nine-week quarters and a large summer vacation. A trend in the eighties and early nineties attempted to maintain the 180-day system, but spread it out through an entire year. This approach meant that after each nine-week quarter, there was a three-week vacation and then a summer vacation that was a little longer than three weeks. School calendars of this type are all based on a system that has been around for a century or more and are far too outdated.

In an Efficient Society, job sharing allows everyone to rotate jobs in all professions on a trimester system. Modeled after most university schedules, public school systems will reflect this trimester system as well. This will also leave room for an increase in efficiency that could allow the division of work time and school time into quarter systems. By providing this correlation of time off, parents and their children will have more time together, education will still be optimally productive, and learning will be even greater because there will be more time to travel and gain knowledge through practical life-experience.

Classification

In the first part of the Efficiency Theory, we are looking at society as the engine of a car and emphasizing that every part of the engine is equally important for it to function efficiently. Though each part is equally valuable for the system's overall efficiency, what we now need to point out is how each part plays a specific role. Certainly, each part is necessary for the vehicle to function, but if the parts are not put in the proper places, their value is diminished, as is the overall function of the vehicle. For example, glass is necessary for the windows, but if we tried to use glass for the bumper, it would be extremely insufficient. We must select where parts should be most appropriately placed in order to make the strongest, most efficient vehicle possible.

This is a highly efficient way of organizing society, but the truth is that for society to work at its highest capacity, some inconvenient facts must be acknowledged, some truths must be accepted, and some freedoms must be taken away. The fact is, people are not created equal and therefore should not be pushed in the same direction. Some people are born with a business intellect while others are born with the ability to quickly learn a trade or craft. However, the way the system is currently set up, we have people who have little or no talent in math pursuing degrees in engineering. We have people running businesses that would be much more efficient saving lives in the medical field. Many times, lack of success eventually separates these people from continuing on an unsuitable path, but it takes time to really establish where their talents are best suited.

Our current system does understand this, but uses the frustrating method of separating these people by the illusion of failure and does not adequately consider the element of passion. Long ago, when I graduated from high school, a friend of mine went to a major university and entered directly into the engineering program. He was miserable as he was faced with a series of grueling classes that he referred to as "weeding classes." These classes are designed to be extremely difficult, with the idea that inapt students will eventually drop out or fail out.

Sure enough, my friend ended up dropping out after one year. The irony was that, several years later, he got a job in computing and has been successfully engineering computer programs for a major newspaper in the southwest for years with a less than adequate education. He has been successful because, though he didn't have the intellect and discipline to make it through the "weeding classes," his desire, interest, and talent in this particular field poured over into personal study of computer programming.

The unfortunate thing about this story is the means by which his success came about. This was certainly the least efficient way for my friend to become an engineer and for years his talents were being wasted. To solve this problem, we need to take a very close look at people's interests, wills, and desires. Students seeking to find their purpose can easily be placed into academies long before university study is required. This is why Efficiency Education is imperative for our social efficiency and overall success.

Within Efficiency Education, we shall implement classifications. Students will be classified based on skill, intelligence, talent, desire, will, and interest. All of these components will be calculated to give them a potential ranking. The school system should be set up in a way that categorizes students based on this score or ranking of their potential. For example, a highly intelligent kid with a tremendous amount of will, interest, and motivation, would be placed into a school with high level classes that relate to his or her area of interest. A student who has high intelligence but lacks interest or motivation, or has the motivation and interest but lacks the intelligence, would be placed in the second tier of schools for further development. These students would be groomed as potentials. The third category, which will have a variety of tiers, will be students who lack interest and intelligence. These students would be placed into the bottom category, and may be groomed as service workers or tested further to find their potential.

This is not a new concept. In fact, as inhumane as this sounds, it is currently taking place all over the world, including the U.S. Privileged students go to privileged schools and disadvantaged students go to disadvantaged schools. The problem is, it is currently based on family wealth and nothing else. We have far too many privileged students wasting space at a privileged school simply because their family is wealthy. That student's seat would be far better suited for a poorer kid who had tremendous talent, intelligence, and desire.

This ranking would become their future place in the professional world. The occupations they will be prepped for will directly correlate with the national salary scale. There will be no, "I don't care about my education, because I can make more money doing something else," attitude. They will see their future in front of them every day. Imagine the motivational power this would have, when students will physically see themselves on the route to a job outside of their passion and living a constant reminder of their future professional track if they do not change something. Some people will be happy on this track, as their passion may be in a $50,000 a year job painting houses, but seeing it right in front of them daily provides a constant reminder of where they will fit in society. If they do not agree with their placement, then they will know what they need to do to change.

As a reflection of this, schools would be set up in a way that distributes students accordingly. Students on the lower-level labor track would be trained primarily in labor skills and trades, and would be disciplined in a way to promote subordination and order. These people are on track to be construction workers, and traditional laborers, and their internships would reflect this. Higher-level groups would be trained to think outside the box, promote business sense, learn highly technical skills, develop leadership, and instill management abilities.

For society to run more efficiently, people must have a clear awareness of where they fit and accept their place in the society. Since education is the at the forefront of the socialization process and plays such a tremendous role in shaping society, it only makes sense for educators to be decisive in setting declarations of student potential. We must face the fact that some people lack motivation and lack professional direction. Some of these people have no plan other than to live off of their mother and father or the government. In an Efficient Society, there are no freebies and the system is blatantly honest. An Efficient Society will not tolerate freeloaders. Capable people, who choose not to utilize the efficient system, will be forced to work, if they do not, they will be imprisoned.

In prisons today, people work against their will and the work gets done. If people do not want to work, they are forced to work. If they still do not work, then they are provided with nothing, just as they have given nothing. No food, no drink, no life. The rationale is simple: if they are not contributing to society then they are a waste to society and a waste of the very resources that keep societal contributors functioning. These people are like a weed growing in a flower patch, it needs to be eliminated, or it will destroy the beauty of the flowers.

Fulfillment Through Teaching

Humans were born to teach. It is our inherit nature to educate one another. From the earliest form of human consciousness to our current status, it has been the goal of humans to learn, pass on what we have learned, and expand on that. We take great pride in passing on what we have learned to someone else: as parents, as friends, as volunteers, and as mentors. Every person on this planet has been a student and a teacher, and people will continue to teach throughout their lives. This is our way of living eternally, by leaving our personal mark on the world. People pass on their personal beliefs and the knowledge they have attained through years of education and experience. Human beings instinctively do this so their spirit will live on through the people they have taught and then through the next generation of people who are taught by those people and so on.

In an Efficient Society, there are two ways of harnessing this productive instinct to teach. One way is to promote, provide, and give preference to the elderly as educators. The second way is to implement knowledge communities.

By promoting the elderly as teachers, we are not saying that someone younger, who is passionate about teaching, will not be just as beneficial as a teacher. Remember, with job sharing there will be more teaching jobs available, and there will be more schools with special academies provided as students are classified by the tier system. Where the elderly will most benefit education will be during the exploratory and skill development years.

Where the inefficient society today would have an engineer, scientist, or doctor retire, an Efficient Society will have them continue expressing their passions as teachers until they are incapable of performing. They have been educated thoroughly in the field; they have the practical experience; and they bring knowledge, skills, and perspective to the classroom that a professionally trained teacher may not have. By doing this we are no longer wasting the great resource elderly people can provide for us (which happens at retirement), but we are also providing incredible knowledge to young learners as they efficiently work together.

Knowledge Communities

One problem with continuing education today is it has become extremely institutionalized, making it far too formal. People attend schools throughout their childhood, attend college, and often forgo further education unless it is required by their employment or if they want to change careers. For the most part, people sincerely enjoy learning new things. There are the occasional stubborn or lazy people who do not want to do anything, but most people like to learn. In today's world, technology is advancing, the world is globalizing, and, whether people like to learn or not, they are being required to learn constantly. However, much of this learning is beginning to come in a more informal educational process. Formats such as workshops and seminars offer all kinds of educational opportunities on various subjects, but more often, it is a friend teaching a friend.

To some, the idea of spending personal or "free time" in an educational setting sounds repulsive. This is because of the unpleasantly formal experiences we have internalized from our early school years. However, many of these same people have no problem attending another form of formal education every Sunday or Saturday. When people attend church or mass, or any other weekly religious sermon, they are essentially going to school. In fact, the American school system was modeled after religious schools. So here I must ask, if people can spend this much time at a religious congregation, learning moral characteristics, why can't we spend a little time learning about life, science, technology, history, or any other pedagogical subject as well.

The knowledge communities will gather at a meeting place where adults and their children can objectively pursue knowledge through shared experience, seminars, symposiums, debates, and experimentation. This vision is modeled after the common western church, where there is a meeting place and scheduled time for various groups to come together in a common interest to pursue knowledge and continue to educate themselves.

Experts will conduct various workshops in every given field, ranging from physics to metaphysics, sociology to anthropology, chemistry, biology, philosophy, religious studies, geometry, engineering, technology, ethics, and so forth. At first, this may be limited since it will depend on membership and member expertise. The goal is to attract as many highly educated people as possible from the local community and, as membership increases, there will be more knowledge and expertise to be shared. The experts would rotate as teachers, allowing multiple perspectives and thoughts on issues and also providing each teacher the opportunity to grow by becoming a student in another field as well.

There would be an opening introduction in a main auditorium where a weekly review of current events, breakthroughs, and any group discussion desired. From there, people would break into subgroups where they can emphasize an area of interest, to learn, discuss, and practice new content.

Example:

8:00 AM: Meeting of the Minds: A gathering of everyone in a common room where announcements will be made. A non-biased weekly review of major world news, religious, political, economical, and scientific issues.

8:30-9:15 AM: Opinion/Debate session on any of the discussed issues.

9:30 AM: Knowledge Sharing: Have you ever thought about the grandest collaboration of life in general? Have you ever thought about the inner working of those things we take for granted the most? What if you could stop wondering and start understanding? Knowledge sharing provides this opportunity.

Church is really just a weekly lesson, taught under a medium (the priest or pastor). Most religious sermons are meant to train people to behave in a certain manner, to control how they perceive the world, and ultimately convince them to follow church doctrine.

I offer the opposite. I offer a medium that assists people in their personal development, by empowering them through knowledge. I truly believe that the unexamined life is not worth living, so I offer a multifaceted form of examination. My philosophy is, people should not be told who they are, what to believe, and what they should strive to be, but instead people should personally discover who they are, what they believe, and what they want to be through knowledge, experimentation, and debate. If we spend our entire lives being pushed in one direction, we will only know what is on that one side.

Five to ten different subjects will be lead in a workshop type atmosphere where people can develop a better understanding and deeper knowledge of a desired subject. Witness and participate in scientific experiments, learn and assist in the development of computer technology, learn psychological statistics and breakthroughs, learn and assist with medical diagnosis and treatments. The potential is limitless. You may discover an expertise that comes easy to you or you may find something difficult but develop a greater appreciation for those who work in the field. Regardless of the gain you seek, knowledge communities provide an endless opportunity for personal growth and knowledge development that can be used while working or during time off.

Families in an Efficient Society

One of the greatest destructive forces in society is the failure of families. Today, we have the largest number of single parent families and uncared for children in the history. The negative effects this has on society are compounded in every facet of the physical, psychological, and social planes of human existence. When we analyze the cause-and-effect relationships of family failure, the results are quite alarming. For every child born out of wedlock, that child is five times more likely to commit a crime and 100 times more likely to have a child out of wedlock him or herself.[48] If the human species is to continue to survive, then progression must be positive.

The law of accelerated returns explains the exponential increase in cause-and-effect relationships. This is an empowering theory in terms of technological advances. However, the theory never addresses what happens if the accelerated returns are negative? Looking at the world and the reproductive fertility in various social subgroups, it can be seen that the groups that are having the most offspring are the groups that are the least educated, least productive, have the most problems, and ultimately are the least efficient.[49] Based on the Law of Accelerated Returns, if these negative aspects of society continue to expand at the exponential rate that they are, society will eventually be subdued by the degenerative factors associated with these offspring.

At a global level, United Nations data reports that the countries where the population is growing at the fastest rate are mostly third world countries in Central Africa, the Middle East, and Indonesia (UN). These are all areas where poverty and conflict is high, education and health care is low, and society is least productive. Domestically this is demonstrated when comparing the number of children born to socio-economically poor parents versus the number of children born to socio-economically affluent parents. The U.S. Census statistics show that over the last thirty years, the rate at which the population is increasing the fastest is in primarily low income, and poorly educated communities.[50]

Also consider that statistically, children who are raised in uneducated, unsupportive, and low-income families are overwhelmingly more likely to become criminals, neglect their own families, and drain more from society than they contribute through systems like welfare. For an Efficient Society to exist, we must fix this problem.[51]

There are many quick fixes that government has tried to implement, but these invariably result in only a temporary change. To change this permanently and be on our way to the most efficient society in history, we need to change to a current "modern" belief about creating and developing a family. In order to even consider something different than what we have always done, people must not look at things in terms of right and wrong based on what we do now, but instead analyze what *works* and *does not work*. There are basically two major issues today that are contributing to the deterioration of the family, 1) the lack of preparation to raise a child, and 2) the rate of divorce.

No matter how much people try, they are rarely prepared for the significant changes that comes with raising a child. Women are at times impregnated by accident and without thorough consideration, and much more often in poor and uneducated parts of the population. People often have a child without really evaluating the responsibilities that come with having a child and the changes a child will create in their lives. No matter how old the person is, unless they have thoroughly investigated the issues concerning parenthood, they will not be prepared.

In an Efficient Society, giving birth is considered a cherished privilege, rather than a carefree or accidental result. Before having a child, future parents will be required to attend a series of classes, which they must complete and validate that they are responsible enough to be a parent. After completing the classes they will receive a legal certificate confirming permission to have a child. Once impregnated, parents will be legally required to attend classes throughout the entire pregnancy that involve parenting, discipline strategies, developmental stages, stress it may cause on the relationship, how to correlate raising a child with their careers (such as, timing job rotations to fit with the child's schooling), and other issues involving child care. Failure to complete the classes will result in a label "Unfit Parent" and they will be not be allowed to parent the child, which may go into adoption or a child-care center until the parent completes the course. The label will be provided on the person's driver's license.

This may sound harsh at first but, seen through the perspective of an Efficient Society, it is very reasonable. In the Efficient Society, there is no reason a couple cannot invest the time it takes to prepare for parenthood. Currently, many couples find time for parenting classes, marriage counseling, and Lamaze classes even with their busy schedules. With Job sharing, there will be more than enough time available and, with the salary system; poverty will no longer be an issue. If a couple truly wants to start a family in an Efficient Society, they will have the wealth, time, and educational opportunities to prepare for and build a strong family that will not burden society but will instead contribute to our social efficiency.

Divorce is another factor that not only contributes to the poor development of children, but also to unhappiness in general. When people's minds are consumed by bothersome circumstances in their family lives, they tend to be less productive, and when people's productivity drops, so does the efficiency of our social whole.[52]

When we look at the main causes for divorce, we can see that when we embrace social efficiency, the divorce rate will decrease also. The Center for Marriage and Family at the Institute for American Values reports that time, money, and sex are the three biggest problems that often lead to an unhappy marriage.[53] Today, our social structure is set up in a manner that compounds these very issues. As we are manipulated to believe we need more money, people work longer hours. This takes time away from the relationship and puts stress on the marriage. People come home from a long day at work stressed out, too exhausted, or lacking the time to spend quality time together.

In the Efficient Society the issues that are known to cause divorce will not exist. Job sharing will give people the time to spend together, benefitting their relationship with their spouse and their kids. The Fair Compensation Act will eliminate the stress money has on so many families, and provide people with opportunities to travel, and do other great things together that they may not be able to afford under our current system. This will decrease the divorce rate. Children will be raised under ideal conditions, which will improve education, decrease crimes and decrease the many other negative effects of torn families have on society. And perhaps most importantly, make people happier.

Solution 5: EliminatE Waste

No More Politics

In the United States, we claim to have superior policies to the rest of the world, and we arrogantly spread our way of democracy across the world. However, while we claim democracy, we have actually become more imperialistic over the last century. Rather than democratically voting on issues, we have leaders doing as they please and justifying why they did so. We continue to have special interests using lobbyists and bombarding us with negative campaign ads to manipulate our vote in order to get what they want. When you really look at how our system is run, we are anything but democratic.

We must understand that politics is completely intertwined with business and wealth. Try to name one president, senator, governor, or any major politician that is from the lower or middle class. If we search, we can find that the salaries of these officials are good, but not completely absurd. The Bureau of Labor and Statistics shows that in 2007, a Governor's salary ranges from $70,000 to $206,500 a year, while Senators and Representatives are paid $174,000 a year.[54] However, their salaries don't reveal the inherent wealth from their families, or their personal wealth through businesses, oil, investments, or former employment. The presidents we have had in recent history have all been multi-millionaires well before they ever became presidents, which is a trait shared in common with many other politicians. Once we have implemented national salary caps and eliminated the greed factor in politics, the fuel behind most dirty politics will be eliminated. Then we will find politicians who genuinely care about providing what is best for our efficiency and for the social whole.

Forget campaign finance reform; in an Efficient Society, campaigning is eliminated altogether. No longer will we be spending hundreds of millions of tax dollars on government marketing. Campaigning is ultimately one politician's sales pitch on why the people should vote for them and not the other person. Unfortunately, just as all manipulative marketing strategies do, these commercials often twist and embellish the facts in an attempt to make one politician look better than they really are just to win the vote. Even worse, the same strategies are applied in the opposite fashion to discredit or make the other politician look bad.

In an efficient system, instead of playing this manipulative game of "he said, she said," the populous will be provided with a single generic and objective information commercial and a pamphlet for each candidate. This will state their history (like doing a background check). It will include everything legal and illegal, good and bad, objectively provide their stance on issues, and outline their beliefs. Rather than having a debate against each other, candidates would be questioned on their policies in a town hall format. The primary objective is to let the voters decide, rather than having television commercials designed to convince people about what to decide.

Political candidates will no longer come from families of wealth who are seeking power and the ability to control the populous. Instead, we will elect professionals and experts in various fields who are passionate about making life more efficient for all. These experts will be from fields such as sociology, biotechnology, philosophy, economics, and other relevant fields. We will also harness the incredible power of the information age and use the internet to vote. When issues are on the table, relevant information will be provided on the internet via informative video clips and written information. A voting window will then be opened for a 24-hour period, via the internet, just like many polls are done already. Online voting would allow ample time for anyone to read up on the issue (which could have a popup that succinctly describes the bill, or official's ideologies) and vote from the comfort of their own home, from their office computer, from a library, or from an internet café. No one will be denied the ability to vote since computers do not discriminate, and votes can be counted in real-time.

There will be in place a checks-and-balances system to prevent poor decisions made in an emotional state by the public. Rather than a singular president having the final say, or a mess of obstacles that occur with multiple branches of government, there will be an expert panel of scholars who will be the final check of approval. They may adjust it for a second vote or veto the initiative altogether, but most importantly; it will no longer be a political game. The experts suggest, the public votes, and the experts approve. Here the system reaches efficiency.

No Retirement

A truly Efficient Society will use all of its resources to the best of its ability, and waste as little as possible. People are a society's top resource and, if people are not contributing, they become a wasteful burden on society. Our current system is set up in such a way that most people have an objective focused on working hard for a good portion of their lives in order to retire comfortably. The average legal age for retirement is now 62 years old, but the government will not grant full Social Security benefits until 67.[55] Interestingly, that the University of Michigan Retirement Research Center found that 43 percent of retirees end up going back to work, and that number is expected to continue to rise for a number of reasons.[56] First of all, most people do not set aside enough money throughout their careers for them to retire comfortably. Secondly, Social Security benefits have been depleted and may not be around anyway, due to the government's misuse of funds and gross underestimates. Third, Medicare is not effectively paying for many of the medical problems people face as they age and their bodies weaken, so they return to work to receive insurance. Our current system promotes retirement, which allows for an enormous number of people to drain from the system without putting anything back into it. The current system says, "Put as much in as you can and then we'll take care of you." But this is not efficient, nor is it what is best for people or for society as a whole.

In an Efficient Society, retirement does not exist. There is a place for everyone to contribute to the overall goal of society. If people are not physically able to perform tasks they once had, they should be using their expertise in a management position or teaching younger people their trade. With technology today, anyone can work from remote locations, use online tools, and have the ability to receive and send resources from anywhere in the world. In today's technologically advanced society, a person could hypothetically work from a retirement home, or even a bed. Currently, we label elderly people as "helpless" and this label not only has an extremely negative effect on them, but also clouds our minds about their true capabilities. Studies have shown that elderly people who work and/or volunteer are generally healthier due to social, psychological, and physical stimulation throughout their days. These studies have also shown that elderly people generally live longer, healthier lives when they continue to work after retirement.[57] An Efficient Society understands the benefits that this delivers both from the productivity that the working elderly can provide to the social whole and for the health and wellness of the person who is working.

Now, if you are having a difficult time with this now because you can't wait to have the free time retirement would have provided, then let me remind you that in the Efficient Society you will be able to experience the wonders of having more free time through out your whole life. By virtue of our new job-share working schedules, we will have been granted the free time to live the joys of retirement throughout our lives, instead of only in the last part of our lives. Through the design of an efficient working system, we will produce more as a whole society, while individually doing less. This means, we will actually have more time for ourselves spread throughout the course of a lifetime, rather than getting several years off in a row during our least capable years.

Imagine having the time to travel the world, exercise, take up a new hobby, and enjoy the wonders of life while you are young and capable rather than old and fragile. Rather than our elderly friends and relatives being miserable at home with nothing to do, they will be still working, socializing, and contributing to a greater cause, thus living a richer, more fulfilling life. By using all of our working resources, including the elderly, we will have achieved a greater balance in society though eliminating the wasted effort, time, and skills that the drain of retirement causes to our system.

The Physically and Mentally Handicapped

In an Efficient Society, we no longer treat people as unequal. We understand that everyone has something to contribute to the advancement of society and the efficiency of our social system. We understand that the elderly, as well as the physically and mentally impaired, can and should contribute. Our current system points out flaws in handicapped people and tells them they are outcasts and incapable of contributing to society. This again drains from our social efficiency by wasting it's number one resource, people. We waste brilliant minds and useful bodies everyday by treating handicapped people as if they are on a lower level than the rest of us. The first thing we need to do is realize that *everyone* can contribute and have an important role in our social advancement. Rather than telling people, "Do nothing and we'll put together programs to take care of you," we need to put them to work where they can be productive. These people are not leaches on society until society and programs provide for them the opportunity to leach off others.

Instead of allowing this, we need to train them to perform tasks of interest within their physical or mental abilities. We are being unbelievably arrogant when we feel we can make a judgment to deem someone useless. We can train circus animals to perform tricks, and we can teach monkeys working skills, but we will deem a handicapped person useless and allow them to be unproductive members of society. This is one of the most disgusting features of our current system. In the Efficient Society, everyone can and will contribute in one way or another. Handicapped people will take advantage of the Efficient Education system just like everyone else. They may or may not be placed at a lower tier based on their ability, desire, and intelligence ranking; but regardless, they will be trained to be productive individuals that contribute to our overall efficiency.

Quite often, people have become physically handicapped through an accident or an unfortunate circumstance, but they still have the complete functioning of their brains. These people should not be set aside and treated like an infant who needs us to care for them; instead, they should be participating in our advancement. They too should be living their purpose and passion. Just as retirees have found, many disabled people have also found that, by staying part of the greater cause, they will live a much happier, healthier, and more normal life.

I remember long ago, when I was in Junior High School, we had a guest come and speak to us at an assembly. The guest was a man who had his legs blown off during the Vietnam War. What was special about his story was that most of the men in his platoon who suffered a loss of ability had become sour at life, stayed at home hiding from the public, and were constantly sick. He was one of the few that decided that nothing was going to hold him back. He went back to college, got a job in marketing, and has lived a much longer and healthier life, while a couple members from his old platoon, who had less physical damage from the war, had actually died. His message was that, when people work and contribute to society, regardless of what society has told them they are capable of, will have purpose— and purpose gives you the will to go on.

I suggest that everyone take a day out of their lives and assist with the handicapped kids at the local school. Except for the extreme conditions, these children want to learn. They want to contribute, and so much of the time, it is the little accomplishments that make these people so proud of themselves. There is a story I was told once about a boy with Down syndrome (we'll call him Andy) who worked as a busboy at a local restaurant. Andy's only job was to take dirty plates from the tables when people were done with them—and he was fantastic. He seemed to have a 6th sense for knowing when people were finished because he was always right there to ask if you wanted him to take your plate, just when you needed him. He became loved by the customers and appreciated by everyone. He always had a smile on his face and took such great pride in cleaning the tables for people. One day a group of regulars were in and they noticed that their plates were not taken immediately after they had finished. Alarmed, they asked the waitress where Andy was. She told them no one was sure what was wrong but he had been rushed to the hospital the night before.

That night after dinner, the group of customers got together and made a plaque that read: "To Andy, The Greatest Busboy Ever." Unfortunately, they were too late and Andy had passed away. When they gave the plaque to Andy's mother, with tears coming from her eyes, she told them, "Before he went unconscious, he asked me to tell the customers at the restaurant that he was sorry for leaving the tables messy."

The point of this story is that most people who seem incapable in the eyes of the general public have a lot to offer society if they are given a chance. We neglect them and tell them they should sit at home because they are of no help, when the reality is we do need them and they will play a vital role in the overall efficiency of society. We must also remember that some of the most brilliant minds of geniuses like Charles Hawkins and Beethoven come from a disabled body. It is time we truly harness the minds and abilities of everyone in our society to bring society to its ultimate efficiency.

There are plenty of jobs that need to be done that few people would chose to do. This doesn't make these jobs any less important for our overall goal of efficiency, rather it reemphasizes that, for society to run efficiently, all jobs need to be completed and all people have an equally important role to play. Some people will find purpose in doing work that others wouldn't care to do. Just as Andy took such pride in cleaning tables, he could just as well have taken such pride in picking up someone's trash. This doesn't make the jobs some people do any less important; their purpose in doing them is just different. It is extremely important for us to realize that all jobs are equally important for society to run efficiently and to realize a greater appreciation for everyone who works.

No More Welfare

Welfare is an example of worst kind of inefficiency. Taken from the socialist philosophy, welfare vows to take care of all people in the fairest way possible by caring for those people who are not working or contributing to society. This creates a huge problem because we are again allowing the system to be drained by people who are not contributing. These people do not have jobs and, as a result, they are reducing our overall efficiency.

Imagine our economic system as an empty bucket. As we work and contribute to the system, we are filling the bucket with water. However, the problem with this bucket is that it is continuously growing as the population grows and we are constantly poking holes in it with programs like welfare, retirement, disabled benefits, and so on. Any time we allow people to suck off the system without putting anything back in; they become holes in the bucket. When we effectively train people, give them jobs, and do not provide programs that allow them to leach off society, we have effectively fixed the leaking holes.

In an Efficient Society, there is no welfare because all people contribute. There is absolutely no reason for anyone to be a drain on society. Even with a 9 to 10 percent unemployment rate in the U.S., you can open any newspaper to the job section and you will find hundreds of jobs available. Do an online search for jobs and you will find thousands more; and these are only the documented jobs. There are thousands more jobs that will never be advertised. We must also take into account the enormous number of jobs that will become available once we embrace efficiency and begin sharing jobs. By simply splitting the jobs that are currently being worked, we will have doubled the employment rate. When our level of economic efficiency allows us to split jobs into thirds, as described in the job sharing section, the effect will be two new openings for every currently-filled job. Every unfilled and newly created position will actually turn into three open positions. We won't have an unemployment rate. Instead, we will have a superfluous number of job vacancies, allowing everyone a place in the most efficiently run system in history.

Implementation and Acceptance

Part of this book's purpose is to help readers become aware of the manipulating influences around them. We are trained to believe that certain social structures are core to our development and propaganda is used to instill belief in these structures. Propaganda influences are everywhere and most people simply accept them. Schools, churches, media, commercials, billboards, and newspapers all bombard us with manipulative messages. So, as I begin to explain what needs to occur to gain acceptance of the Efficiency Theory and to implement it, I do so with transparency and openness rather than hidden manipulation.

While the delivery methods used to communicate social changes may be just as manipulative, this can be mitigated by open acknowledgement. For example, if any society's methods of attaining agreement involve coercion, force, or subliminal messages, people are being manipulated. But if you tell people what they are being taught and why, then people have the choice to believe and maintain individual trust from an objective perspective. This is not happening now because the public has such little trust in the all-powerful social institutions that govern us that authorities must continue to find stronger and more indirect ways of manipulating the masses. Unfortunately, because of the lack of trust, these same indirect strategies must initially be used until the benefits of efficient systems are seen. Once society begins to run more and more efficiently, trust will be restored in the system, and manipulative methods will be unnecessary.

To begin, the manipulative methods used today will have to be applied simply because they are the only effective way to inform the majority of people. People can't simply be taught something and have it effectively make sense to them. In the book *Influencer,* the authors explain that the best way for people to learn is through experience but, when that experience is not available, they learn best through "vicarious experience."[58] This is why story telling, television, and radio are so powerful at influencing people. They provide this vicarious experience that people need in order to understand a concept better. Therefore, we must include television, radio, and music to effectively implement the Efficiency Theory's strategies.

In doing so, we must also eliminate money-motivated political radio and television, which essentially fills people's minds with completely biased and greed-driven agendas, often backed by lobbyists or financial groups. These figures are able to stir emotions and cause social conflict because they know the public is generally too lazy to research issues and draw their own conclusions on issues. So people turn to political media sources that give a biased analysis of problems and tell the public what they want us to believe.

Instead, we must show researchers on the media screen knowledgeably discussing the issues. A host should not broadcast their own opinions, but interview experts to present facts. We must teach history truthfully by spending more time teaching present issues and showing how they correlate with history. We must emphasize causes and effects and how what we are do-

ing now could affect the future. There are many infer-
ences that can be drawn from history to shed light on
where current issues are leading society. These issues
need to be taught and pondered. We need to awaken
the minds of developing generations to important issues concerning the present and future, along with
various potential positive and negative plans of action
and the possible results of those actions. We need to
challenge the young to visualize their futures to foresee
problems and correct them before they occur.

Media and education can only take us so far in the
implementation process. Support must come from all
avenues of life, because beliefs are developed in the
home, in schools and in religious institutions as well.
Once these beliefs become common, the process of
implementation becomes easier. For example, if people
believe life will be better when the majority of power
is taken away from the rich-elite and distributed more
evenly, only then will they be willing to implement a
nationwide salary scale. However, as long as people are
content with the rich making the decisions, our present
situation will continue. When people believe a board of
intellectuals and scholars can lead us in a better direction than money-motivated political figures, then we
can implement a better form of leadership. And when
people believe in a school system that will assist them
and guide them to their most fulfilling place in life, then
they will cherish the education they receive. The implementation of an Efficient Society will ultimately come
from within.

Chapter 6
If We Do Not Change

Our Collapse

There have been many civilizations throughout history that have developed into extremely powerful, prosperous, and efficient societies. They learned to work with their environments, using nature and natural phenomenon to make life easier, while working together and trading with each other in an extremely efficient manner. However, it is also important to realize that even these seemingly efficient societies eventually perished. If we analyze these societies thoroughly, what we find is they share a single common trait that contributed to their downfall. Greed invariably created the problems they faced; but their obstinate unwillingness to adjust to the extreme changes and demands of their societies ultimately led to their collapse.[59]

Like us, most civilizations are fruitful and prosperous during stable, plentiful, and desirable conditions. However, once conditions become unpleasant and resources become scarce, the stability of a civilization is shaken and tumultuous times are imminent. There is evidence of this phenomenon in the ancient Mesoamerican, Viking, and Polynesian civilizations. This has also become evident in more recent times, for example, in Haiti, in parts of Africa, and even in the U.S. when crime spikes as people become frustrated and angered by their place in society.

We are at such a crucial time in modern civilization. We are surrounded by all of the classic causes for societal collapse. Environmental problems, depletion of resources, economic instability, and religious upheaval have all historically become the roots of social demise. We face all of these extremely challenging problems today. As every other great civilization in history discovered, without adjustment of our social system, we will become extinct.

Our history is littered with incredible civilizations whose empires crumbled and whose societies fell apart. In our vast arrogance, we consider these societies primitive and discount their relevance to us today. We need to wake up and realize that we are not immune to destruction. We are fully aware of why these previous civilizations collapsed, yet we continue to follow in their footsteps. Unless we take action, we will meet the same destiny as previous great societies. We must improve our efficiency to survive.

Chapter 7
Global Efficiency

Resources

On a global level, competition over resources is one of the greatest causes of social problems, past, present, and future. War after war has been fought with the direct, or indirect, agenda of controlling land that contains desired resources. Whether the conflict dates back to early battles over territories rich in gold, or present day battles over territories rich in oil, the cause remains the same. Each of the 193 nations is ultimately concerned with the preservation, protection, and furtherance of their own interests. Nations will kill the populations of other nations and sacrifice their own people in battle to fulfill this selfish agenda.

However, a battle is only necessary when the resources are in short supply and a nation needs them. To prevent ourselves from completely destroying each other, we developed international trade organizations. With global trading, we can provide nations with very little resources access to needed resources without a military dispute. When a nation is unable to trade resources, we have ingeniously developed ways to trade labor, brain-power, and/or manufacturing capabilities in place of resources. However, for this to occur effectively, we must get each nation to buy into the same program and agree to the terms. In theory, this is a perfect set up, but we must not forget that business is business. As long as there is a feeling of separation, such that we must take from each other in order to build ourselves up, it will be impossible to have a completely effective program.

While people continue to believe in the illusion of ownership, they will continue to be stricken by the negative effects of greed. When we are not happy with someone, we will cut them off. When we feel cheated, we respond by cheating someone else. Because of this condition, our global trade organizations have actually produced one of the most dangerous strategies ever developed, the perfect storm of political power through greed and wealth.

When we begin to analyze the consumption of resources on a global level, we can better evaluate the situation and become much more efficient societies. As a national community, we look at our land and build a great nation from the pieces we bring together from different parts of the country. In the U.S., we have states and territories that provide us with specific resources. For example, the coastal states primarily provide sea resources, business trading, and tourism, the mountain states primarily provide mining and agriculture, and winter recreation, the plains states primarily provide agriculture, and the Midwest primarily provides manufacturing. Ultimately, we merge these pieces together to provide for the entire nation. However, no single nation is efficient enough. Even with all of its resources, the U.S. still imports more than it exports. What this shows us is that efficiency is not that simple. This is because the U.S. market economy has placed business profit ahead of efficiency. Industries would rather make a quick buck than prepare an infinitely more perfect future for the people.

Globally, there is no doubt that there are enough resources in the world for everyone to live comfortably, and scientific technology is making more resources available and improving the ease of production each year. Imagine the possibilities of a global community that worked together as a single nation, rather than as separate battling entities. Imagine the efficiency of more than 6 billion people on the same page, working toward the same purpose. Imagine the peaceful pleasure of living in a global community where people care for one another and where everyone works towards the universal goal of human development.

Nearly everything in the Efficiency Theory could be applied to a globally efficient whole as well. Currently, there is a renewed interest in getting a human presence on Mars. We will undoubtedly have human beings on Mars within the next hundred years, but if all nations worked together, it could happen in half the time. This level of cooperation is necessary because global conditions are reaching the point where we need each other more than ever. As the human species becomes threatened by depleting planetary resources, we need to work together to engineer new resources or to go beyond our planet to find new resources. This may sound like science fiction, but fifty years ago hybrid vehicles, laptop computers, digital communication, virtual reality, and even the Internet were considered science fiction.

The Law of Accelerated Returns states that, at the current level of expansion, our technology will double every five years, and grow exponentially faster as each technological advance paves the way for further advances. When society comes together on a globally-oriented structure and humanity combines for a singular purpose, this level of efficiency will expand beyond our current comprehension. Global efficiency will work as a catalyst for the incredible technological advances we have already seen, and science fiction will be at our doorsteps.

Tapping into Global Efficiency

Experts have estimated that a single human brain can process 30 to 40 times more information than the most powerful computers of our time. So why is it that computers seem to do more work than most humans? We have over 6 billion human super computers on this planet and well over half of them are wasted, due to inefficient use.

One reason for our incapacity to unite in a coordinated production of human progress is the innate desire to believe that we, as individual entities, are somehow better than others. The truth is, equality is not something that is feared only by persons of power; equality is a problem each and every one of us faces. Even the poorest, most degraded individuals in a society find a way to justify why they are better than someone else.

Why do you think the worst fighting occurs in the poorest neighborhoods and poorest countries? Sure, it's because many of these people are less educated, jealous, and hateful of the privileged, but that doesn't explain why the poor fight the poor. If it were simply about jealousy and hate, then the rich would be the targets. Fighting among the poor is because of an internal fight for social pride, or what most gang members and other social outcasts would call "respect." However, in this usage, "respect" is nothing more than a term used to label one person as better than another.

It is disgusting to hear the fear some Americans have for China's economic and scientific potential. In a globally Efficient Society, we would embrace one another and even assist other nations in their advancement. A globally Efficient Society would collaborate on fuel efficiency, on environmental efficiency, and on creation or discovery of new fundamental resources. This world is full of brilliant minds, but many people are not thinking outside of the box. Instead replanting trees, why aren't we creating a substitute for wood? Instead of trying to figure out where to put all of the garbage, why aren't we trying to figure out how to reuse the garbage? We know that, when garbage rots, it releases methane gas. Why are we not providing chambers that can accelerate the process and store this gas? And perhaps we can develop engines that run on this source of energy. We are worried that our fresh water supplies are running low, but we are not creating new sources of producing fresh water. Instead, we focus on fear of what might come. This stems from our root desire to be in control. Many people may get a sense of safety from suppressing others because they feel as though they are above them, but this could eventually result in our overall global collapse.

Global Prosperity

We have spent centuries, and even millennia, trying to better ourselves. The personal ambition to be labeled "the best" has required us to separate ourselves from each other. We do this through status symbols given by education, economics, religion, racial classifications, and other phenomena that have become an impediment to our evolution. Consider this fact: people are really no different from a cell. We have the same functions and the same parts that make up our physical existence. A cell has the equivalent of a circulatory and respiratory system, a heart, a brain, and so forth. A single cell has the ability to function on its own and still does so today. However, billions of years ago, cells discovered that they could bind together to create a stronger and more efficient cell colony. This allowed cells to spend less effort on surviving and more effort on specialized services. By allowing cells to specialize individually, the whole community of cells became stronger and more efficient.

The next step in this evolutionary process is the combination of cell communities, which bind together to become even stronger than their previous communities. As a result, these communities of cells are able to work together efficiently to produce of an overall or-

ganic structure. Today, we recognize this biological process in all life forms, but the most advanced life form
is a human. A human body is literally a massive cluster
of cell communities that work together for the efficient
function of their specific purposes (for example, blood,
functioning to supply nutrients and oxygen throughout the body), and also for the purpose of the entire
system, the survival of the body.[60]

Evolution has been stuck at this stage for quite
some time. The biological system has made leaps and
bounds in the systematic upgrade from animal to human, but the system has not advanced in a long time.
One reason for this may be the idea that we think we
are strong enough as individuals. We have made some
minimal advances of a kind mirroring our cellular development. For example, there are communities of people
that work together to achieve a more efficient whole.
On a small scale, we call these families or tribes, and
on a larger scale, we call these nations. However, the
prime advancement from this point forward will occur
only when the national community clusters can come
together as one.

The best comparison is to see the world as a human body. Countries are like organs, but we are not
functioning for the whole. Within countries, we see individual cells that act like cancers. They fight, destroy, and
try to exert personal growth against the system, rather
than working together for the benefit of the system as
a whole. These cancers destroy the system and, as a result, the organs (countries) do not work harmoniously
toward the evolution of the whole. Instead, countries

try to promote themselves as better than the whole. However, when we look at the human body, is the liver any less important than the heart? Is the stomach less important than the lungs? When an organ grows too large, it can cause problems in the body as a whole.

The function of society is to work together for the better good of humanity. If people are like the cells of the world body, and countries are like the organs, then we need to work together, as the body does, for the common goal of evolution. Humans will not advance until we come to this realization. Like the cancer that kills the human body, we are killing our world body by not binding together for a common purpose. The purpose is the promotion of the whole.

Chapter 8
The Future is Now

Most people would agree that they would like to live in a more efficient society. People are tired of the wars, the pains, the deaths, the fear, and the negativity that is engulfing this planet. We are ready for a change, but most of the people who read this will not believe it is possible. They will say: "The rich won't accept this and no one will go through with it. It is in our genes to compete with each other, to exploit each other, and to advance ourselves even at the expense of others." This is the belief that many people currently hold and it is this very belief that perpetuates the problems.

My point is, policies cannot change a society. No laws or government can create a harmonious society. Harmony is a frame of mind. It is an understanding and a belief that is put into action. Through thousands of years of war and conflict, people have concluded that harmony is impossible and that peace is a dream. I am here to share with you the good news that you and I, we together are in control of the future. Our thoughts and our beliefs are what make anything possible and no one can control these but us.

Picture this: Tens of thousands of soldiers along the Israeli border are forced into battle by their governments because for thousands of years they have been taught to hate each other because they each believe they are the rightful owners to a piece of land. As heavily armed Israeli tanks approach a neighborhood, the soldiers find something different. There is no resistance. Instead, there are piles of weapons laying in the streets and signs in Hebrew and Arabic that say, "Welcome my brothers and sisters. I will no longer fight. For when you die, a piece of me dies and when I die, a piece of you dies. Please, come in for a drink and stay awhile. My home is your home, and you and I are one."

Many of the troops are suspicious, but they take the chance. Sure enough, would-be soldiers find themselves sitting together in the poverty stricken homes of local families and sharing with them the little that they have. The commander of the army is so moved by the gesture that he responds by inviting the residents to come to the soldier's homes and share what they have. While the older Palestinians are shy about accepting, the commander manages to persuade a few male elders to join them so they can receive some food and shelter from their side. This begins an incredible new era.

The walls, be they physical or in our minds, were put up to separate us, and these walls between peoples make us more inefficient. These walls must fall. The borders of what is currently called Israel or Lebanon, Iraq or Iran, Europe or Russia, Asia or America, exist only in our minds. Where we have defined separation by oceans or mountain, colors and creeds, as we learn the efficiency of unity, we will no longer be separated in thought. There will be no passports, no foreign trade, and no foreign currencies, because we will be one efficient social entity working together for the betterment of humankind. The principle of Occam's razor holds true. The most complex problems often have the simplest answers.[61] The answer to finding peace and harmony is to find *efficiency*. And the only way we can do that is to *change our minds*, *believe* it is possible, and *act* on those beliefs.

Notes

1. http://dictionary.reference.com
2. A. H. Maslow, "A Theory of Human Motivation," Psychological Review, 50(4) (1943): 370-96.
3. http://web.worldbank.org/WBSITE/EXTERNAL/ DATASTATISTICS/0,,contentMDK:20399244~men uPK:1504474~pagePK:64133150~piPK:64133175~ theSitePK:239419,00.html
4. John Kay, "Chaotic Evolution Defines the Market Economy," The Financial Times, 4 November 2009.
5. http://www.un.org/en/development/progareas/ statistics.shtml
6. http://www.cauxroundtable.org/index. cfm?&menuid=126&parentid=52
7. http://www.ilo.org/global/About_the_ILO/Me- dia_and_public_information/Press_releases/ lang—en/WCMS_071326/index.htm
8. Melanie Klein, "Our Adult World and its Roots in Infancy." Human Relations, Vol. 12, No. 4 (1959): 291-303.
9. Vallerand, Robert J. "On Psychology of Passion: In Search of What Makes People's Lives Most Worth Living." Canadian Psychology. Vol. 49, No. 1, 1-13. 2008.

10. Neal E. Miller, "Studies of fear as an acquirable drive: I. Fear as motivation and fear-reduction as reinforcement in the learning of new responses." Journal of Experimental Psychology: General. Vol. 121(1) (Mar 1992): 6-11.

11. Louise Brightwell Miller and Betsy Worth Estes, "Monetary Reward and Motivation in Discrimination Learning," Journal of Experimental Psychology, Vol. 61(6) (June 1961): 501-504.

12. Robert A. Rescorla and Richard L. Solomon, "Two-Process Learning Theory: Relationships Between Pavlovian-Conditioning and Instrumental Learning," Psychological Review, Vol. 74(3) (May 1967): 151-182.

13. P. Smith and R. Curnow, "Arousal Hypothesis and the Effects of Music on Purchasing Behavior," Journal of Applied Psychology, Vol. 50 (June 1966): 255-286.

14. J. Alpert and M. Alpert, "Music Influences on Mood and Purchases Intentions," Psychology and Marketing, Vol.7, No. 2 (Summer 1990): 109-133.

15. Icek Ajzeck, "Theory of Planned Behavior," Organizational Behavior and Human Decision Process: Theories of Cognitive Self-regulation, (50)(2) (December 1991): 179-211.

16. Harvey A. Kaplan, "Greed: A Psychoanalytic Perspective," Psychoanalytic Review, 78 (1991): 505-523.

17. Richard M. Ebeling, "Freedom Daily: The Impossibility of Socialism." The Future of Freedom Foundation, 1990.

18. Edward L. Deci, "The Effects of Contingent and Non- contingent Rewards and Controls on Intrinsic Motivation," Organizational Behavior. (1972): 217-229.

19. Amitav, Chakravarti and Xie, JinHong. "The Impact of Standards Competition on Consumers: Effectiveness of Product Information and Advertising Formats." Journal of Marketing Research. (2006). 1-32.

20. Iris Bohnet and Richard J. Zeckhauser, "Social Comparisons in Ultimatum Bargaining," Scandinavian Journal of Economics, Vol. 106, No. 3 (September 2004): 495-510.

21. Dalai Lama, The Universe in a Single Atom: The Convergence of Science and Spirituality,: Broadway, 2006.

22. Mario Livio, The Golden Ratio: The Story of PHI, the World's Most Astonishing Number, Broadway, 2003.

23. O. Jon Ebbert, T. Ivana Croghan, et al., "Association Between Respiratory Tract Diseases and Secondhand Smoke Exposure Among Never Smoking Flight Attendants: a Cross-sectional Survey," Environmental Health, v6:28, 2007.

24. David A. Baldwin, "Money and Power," Journal of Politics, (Vols. 1-67) 1971.

25. Dispenza, Joe. "Evolve Your Brain." Health Communications Inc. Deerfield Beach, Fl. 2007.

26. http://www.livescience.com/strange-news/060124_political_decisions.html

27. http://educateyourself.org/fe/radiantenergys-
     tory.shtml
28. http://www.haarp.net
29. http://query.nytimes.com/gst/fullpage.html?res
     =9E05E6D71F38F937A35757C0A9669D8B63&sec
     =&spon=&pagewanted=all
30. Thomas L. Friedman, The World is Flat: A Brief His-
     tory of the Twenty-First Century, Washington: Far-
     rar, Straus and Giroux, 2005.
31. Gruber, Jonathan and Wise, David A. "Social Secu-
     rity Programs and Retirement Around the World:
     The Relationship to Youth Employment." National
     Bureau of Economic Research. 2010. 330-335
32. http://www.divorceforum.org/cau.html, 2009.
33. R. C. Engs, Alcohol and Other Drugs: Self Respon-
     sibility, Bloomington, IN: Tichenor Publishing
     Company, 1987.
34. http://www.time.com/time/health/arti-
     cle/0,8599,1903838,00.html
35. http://www.payscale.com
36. http://center.americanvalues.org
37. Karl Marx and Friedrich Engels, Manifesto of the
     Communist Party, International Publishers, 1948.
38. http://www.businessweek.com/news/2010-03-
     09/u-s-millionaires-ranks-rose-16-in-2009-study-
     says-update1-.html
39. http://www.rferl.org/content/Forbes_Rich_List_
     Number_Of_New_Billionaires_Reflects_Global_
     Recovery/1980413.html
40. http://www.nasa.gov/centers/ames/
     pdf/80660main_ApolloFS.pdf

41. http://thebreakthrough.org/blog/2009/07/40th_
     anniversary_of_the_moon_l.shtml
42. http://www.fbi.com. 2009